# JUMP ROPE

## Tara Felina

PAGE PUBLISHING, INC.
New York, NY

First originally published by Page Publishing, Inc. 2018

ISBN 978-1-64214-314-0 (Paperback)
ISBN 978-1-64214-315-7 (Digital)

Printed in the United States of America

Dedicating a book is not easy. I feel it's reserved for someone who has been there for the writer during the entire process. My dedication is simple. When life leads you down a road and you hit a fork, which way do you go? These men have helped me. No, we don't talk on the phone or have weekly coffee. They have helped me through their music. Through moments when I wanted to end it all, moments when I wanted to shout it from the rooftops, moments when I celebrated in silence, moments when I broke down and sobbed from the broken soul within. My arms aren't full of visible marks, but the scars run deep. My heart is sad, even on the best days of being loved by a man who has never laid a hand on me, which wasn't loving.

There is one thing that gets me through all my depression and anxiety, through all the self-doubt and worry.

Dear, Justin, Ryan, Matt, Matthew and Jeremy, little did you know that when we met, I was extremely sad and depressed. I put on a smile as I spoke to each one of you with my husband, thanking you for being there for me.

Justin, I teared up when we spoke and you took my hand.

That night, I got lost in all the words you spoke, and a sense of calm washed over me. You continue to keep me going, and every day I am so thankful to be a part of the Blue Family.

# Just a Girl with a Story to Tell

Hello, my name is . . . wait, hold on. My name is Harry, Harry the Angel. I am not really an angel, you see; I am more of a being that was trapped here on earth since I was a complete asshole growing up. I died, of course, and well, here I am. Why am I talking to you? This is easy. I have been stuck on this earth for about thirty-four, almost thirty-five, years. I died in a hospital, and that was where I met this young lady on the day she was born. I decided to follow her around a bit and some of the shit she went through. I figured, I better let someone know before she does something stupid.

The insane thing is, she isn't crazy, not even a little bit. She does stupid shit because she is human, but she isn't a bad person. She is just a girl who, for whatever circumstances that happens to her, takes life for what it is and keeps plowing. I would have plowed my head straight into the bottle. Guess that's why I am here talking to you instead of in heaven. Oh well.

Are you ready to hear this story? I would start at the day she was born, but up until the time she was in the sixth grade, her life had been normal. Her parents divorced when she was six, but other than that, she was a happy girl. She played outdoors, went camping, and did slip-and-slides during the summer Her dad thought it would be grand to put a slip-n-slide in the ice plant. She was stung by bees. Her dad wasn't an asshole but, like her, did stupid shit. She loved her dad with all her heart. This, however, isn't about her dad. No, this is more about what happened to her and how it changed her entire life. I just think the memory of her getting stung on the slip-n-slide on the ice plant was classic. Again, I'm an asshole.

Back to my main gal, my partner in crime, even though she doesn't know she is. I look at her as still water, calm, peaceful, and then one day, someone threw a giant stone at her.

Think about it. If you throw a stone into still water, what does it do? Someone threw a giant stone in her still water, and this is the woman she became.

She lives and has always lived in California, San Diego to be exact. She feels she doesn't belong here. A lot of people who meet her say they remind her of someone who was from the Midwest or even East Coast. It's because she's not fake. She's not rude, but what you see is what you get. She has many amazing qualities, but one of her biggest downfalls is her constant ability to get stepped on. It wasn't until she was thirty-two that she realized she doesn't have to be stepped on, but it even took a few years after that to follow her own advice.

I have been trying to tell her for years to speak up, but she can't hear me. So I watch in silence and judge her. I'm an asshole; I can do that.

She was born into a "normal" family. She has a mom and dad who both worked for good companies. They weren't wealthy, but their jobs did pay the bills and allowed them to live in a safe neighborhood. She went to good schools and grew up in a small town. She has a brother who is four years younger than her. They are as different as night and day. She believes that if events in her life didn't take place, she and her brother would have similar life paths; however, God always has a plan, and as sick and twisted this plan for her was, I finally understood where she fit.

Her parents divorced when she was six. I personally don't remember the divorce, and I don't remember the things which were said between her parents when they split. I do remember both attempting to raise both her and her brother in a civil environment. They did well for the most part. I know she loved her parents. She wanted to grow up and be like her mother. She thought her mom was "perfect." She was always there and looked and dressed nice. Her mom wasn't into drugs or alcohol. She was the middle child and had to deal with what that feels like. Her mom took them shopping and out to eat. She didn't cook much, or it was from a box. She loved movies, and they went to church on Sundays. Her mom would make sure the holidays were nice; they had a lot of fun and went on a ton of vacations. Her dad was Mr. Outdoors. Every night that they were with him, he cooked them a meal every night that didn't come from a box. They all pitched in to do chores, and during the summer, they played outside ALL day, and sometimes late into the night. There wasn't a thing called TV, or what they watched was minimal. Her parents were extremely different. This is how she was made. This is what made her into the amazing creature she is today.

She is sensitive and very emotional like her mom. She is strong like her dad. Sometimes she is a wrecking ball and a force to be messed, with but she is one hell of a person. Her dad taught her that life happens, and you push forward and don't quit, ever. Her mom taught her that when life happens, you continue to play the victim and just give up. She wouldn't really use the word victim; however, it's the best way to describe her entire family on her mom's side. As harsh as that sounds, her family betrayed her at every turn, which made her confused growing up and seeing friends having these amazing relationships with their families. At the age she is now, she is still learning to trust and let go of those who hurt her, in which letting go hurt just as badly as the betrayal. Are you ready to hear her story? Here goes nothing.

She used to shit herself and she never knew why, until she was an adult and realized it wasn't her fault. Her parents never took her to be seen for her problem. Her mom would make her wash her underwear until she learned to throw them away. She learned why she did this and did grow out of it not long after it began. What she didn't grow out of, however improved, is her self-confidence. Even at the age she is now, her self-confidence is something that is constantly worked on. No matter in life how great things get, something fucks it up, and she starts from square one. As a child, she would walk with her head down, eyes to the ground.

This behavior started early on, after her mom had remarried and went on her honeymoon.

She and her brother stayed at their grandparents' house. These were her mom's parents. Her dad's parents died when she was a baby. When she was at her mom's parents, I remember clearly what happened to change the course of her life, forever her life, or her perspective on life. Her mom's dad molested her. There is no easy way to say it, so there you go. He played with her lady bits. However, he only got so far as to shove his hands down her pants and up her shirt to fondle her breasts, which unfortunately developed at a young age. I know she was confused at what was going on, and I knew that she didn't like how it made her feel. I watched her struggle to break free as he held her on his lap; he wouldn't let her go. She eventually fought him off, and of course, she got in trouble for drawing blood. She bit him hard. I was trying to think back to what she did to make him do such a thing. I remember she was just sitting on his lap. I remember she was wearing blue pajama pants and watching television. I remember she would turn herself around, trying to squirm free, and she was able to bite him; and that's when he called her names, threw her off, and ran to her grandmother for assistance.

Her grandmother cleaned up the blood and then told her, "No one will believe you if you tell." Her grandmother told her this even before she could even say what happened. Her grandmother told her mother what "she" had done when her mother came to pick her brother and her up. I can tell that her mom was confused because she wasn't a biter; however her mom scolded her on the drive home. I, being an asshole angel, don't have many feelings; but that day, I looked out the window and tried not to cry, and I know she was doing the same thing. This hurt my soul, even though I don't think I had one anymore. I wanted so to scream out to her mom, but we all knew her grandmother was law. No one went against her, and that was that. My poor sweet girl will now be who she is for the rest of her life because of selfish people. Fuck them.

I began to push the memory of the molestation to the back of my mind, and I know she had to as well. We both had to learn to forget it due to no one going to believe her, and me not being alive to advocate for her. I know she hated to go over to her grandparents' house, but she did. She put on her happiness, and like turning on the water in the kitchen, it flowed. She was told not to say anything, so she didn't. I still hear people question why this still bothers her. "It only happened once" or "You were able to fight him off." To her, I know the physical trauma went away over time—well, not really; she still has an issue when she is intimate and her breasts are fondled. The bigger trauma was the emotional and the betrayal. It was burned into her memory that she did something wrong and that she was to never tell.

Let's continue to grow up, shall we? I think I left off after the attack. I will continue to jump ahead and move back because there are explanations that need to be said, or different memories that need to be placed. I want her to know it wasn't her fault. None of it. I want her to know that people love and care about her, always.

Summer ended, and she was starting junior high. I was excited for her to start seventh grade. She would get to change different classes, and I was excited for her to make new friends. She played soccer. She made a few friends on the soccer team. She was awful but still had fun playing. She had the biggest crush on this guy who was good. He was cute, so she tried to show off a few times to him, but nothing worked. There were two girls on the soccer team whom she became friends with. She thought they were so "cool." I look back now and realize the two of them used her for their own laughs. They used to have sleepovers. She slept over at both of their houses. They used to leave when everyone was sleeping and go ding dong ditch. They thought they were awesome. There were times they tried to light their own shit on fire in a paper bag. They made her shit in the bag. It never worked, and she pissed herself. It was so late at night, so she couldn't go home, and of course, the girl who lived in the house she stayed at wouldn't give her a change of clothes. The friendship with the two of them ended abruptly. One of her "friends" moved away, which split them up. I liked that. I didn't like those girls. She did meet another girl who was pretty rad. They hit it off well. When she would spend the night at her house, they would take her moped and attempt to hit the tops of mailboxes off with a bat. I felt like every time she did that she was hurting someone who had done her wrong. She thought she was just being a kid. I'll let her to continue to believe that. She needed it.

During the school year in health class, they were watching a video on a sexual assault. Her teacher kept telling them that if someone touches you inappropriately, tell someone. I know she tried so many times but couldn't. She kept pushing it deeper and deeper down. I continued to recall every second of the day what her grandmother had said. I know she couldn't focus; she didn't know what to do or where to turn. She had now been betrayed by three adults who were family, which made her think that family didn't matter. She tried to escape; however, she was the kid who was always caught before she could do something. She believes it was God telling her that he is watching out for her and that he won't ever allow her to get into a situation she couldn't get out of. I tried telling her that there is no God, because if there was, why did he continue to allow her to get screwed for years? She had other ideas in her head. Her faith, man, that is some crazy shit. Not being able to see something or someone but still believing. I guess you can say that I am a little crazy, because if she were able to feel me or see me at all, she would be in the loony bin.

Why, though, did her family do this to her? During school that year, she made a friend, and to this day, I don't remember her name; I don't think she remembers either. I do remember she was rough around the edges. She wore jeans and a flannel shirt, and in the seventh grade, that meant she was tough. She didn't judge her for the way she dressed (I thought she dressed cool too). This friend and she would pass notes in class. During class, this math teacher (whom she hated) confiscated the note. She begged the teacher not to show her mom because it spoke about drinking and wanting to watch the next fight at school. It never said that she did drink or fight. At this point, she had never had a drink in her life, and the fights were always broken up before she got there, but she knew that just the act of writing about such things would get her in trouble.

She arrived home with me in tow, and her mom lectured her about fighting and drinking. Her mom attempted to speak to her about the note she was given. Her mom told her that hanging out with people like her friend wouldn't lead her to anywhere but down. Her mom didn't know that her friend didn't have anything to do with her current behavior or thoughts. She began to really dislike her mom. She didn't hate her, but she was trying to understand why a parent wouldn't protect their child, and that was the only thing she held on to until she became an adult. To be honest, I was thinking the same thing. Little did we both know that this would be a never-ending battle up, until the time she was an adult; and even then, she would still fight for just a simple thing. An apology. To this day, I am unsure why she only wanted an apology, but this was her, she just wanted someone to acknowledge what was done. I did notice she survived seventh grade without a scratch because she wasn't a bad kid; she just wanted to forget what happened to her. She and I were both excited to start eighth grade year with her friends and have a new beginning for herself. Or so we both thought.

During the drive to the vacation spot that summer, I was daydreaming about when I would earn my wings finally and get off this stinking planet when I overheard her asking her mother what sort of activities the family would be participating in that summer. Instead of telling my excited girl, her mother announced that she would be going to private school for the eighth grade and that they wore uniforms. Awesome. Her mom was worried she was heading down a wrong road and wanted to stop it before it began. I really hate this bitch, and from the looks of it, so did she. I knew she didn't want to go to private school or wear ridiculous uniforms. Except for the reasoning of why her mom was sending her to private school, she enjoyed it; she met one of the greatest guys you will ever meet and made some pretty awesome female friends.

During the eighth grade year, she learned a lot about herself. First off, she was the transfer kid—okay, not that far off; she did go to the church, but she felt that she had to learn all over again how to act and conduct herself. She was about twenty-five pounds overweight, with braces and this awful hair, which she put on top of her head with a scrunchy hair tie. She was a wreck. She did like the school though. She made a few friends whom she still sees, though not as much as she likes—you know, doing all that adult stuff. The school had a mandatory sports program, as well as camps. I know she did enjoy it. She was a part of something honest and was building herself confidence in most areas, but one. She still couldn't understand how her mom wasn't like the rest. A lot of her friends complimented her on how pretty her mom was and how fun. Yes, she was pretty and fun; and no, her mom didn't abuse her, which later down the road, she threw in her face like it was a privilege not to have been abused by her. She and her brother were well cared for. They lived in a nice house and had a lot of fun opportunities kids their ages couldn't do. They traveled and had lots of fun. Look, I know that I said. I am an asshole, and I just happened to be there when this little girl came to be, but I chose her. I saw something special in her and, even as an adult, still protecting her from falling face first. I am very honest when I say she did appreciate all the opportunities that was handed to her as a child, even with all the crap that she went through. She knows how lucky she was to experience things she unfortunately can't give her own children, but that is not what she wanted. She wanted her mom to stand up for her. She just wanted her to say "I'm sorry I didn't do anything. What do you want me to do to fix this?"

She, of course, didn't get that response, ever. The first time the molestation was brought up was right after the incident. The second time the topic of molestation was brought up was when her mom was snooping in her room. She had found her journal, which had supposedly opened to the exact page of what she had written. I know she didn't want to write what had happened, but I personally believe her soul was eating her. Normally she wouldn't write down anything as incriminating as this, but during the free writing time of class that day, they were told that they could write anything. They just had to complete it. If the class didn't want anyone reading what they wrote, they could write at the top of the page: *Please don't read.* As simple as that. We both thought her words were safe. I knew her teacher hadn't read it, or if he did, nothing was said. If he did read it and didn't say anything, I may do some haunting for not speaking up. She wrote and left it as is. To her, that was the first time she would speak about the molestation. It was one sentence: *When I was in the 6th grade, my grandfather molested me.* To her, it was a weight lifted, even if it was just her reading it.

I remember driving to her friend's house one day. Like I said, she was making friends in this school—friends her parents approve of and will drive to their houses. On the way over, her mom began to talk about something serious when we both realized what it was. She began to explain that she found her journal, and I was getting hopes up for my sweet girl. *Yes! This is it.* The truth will be out once and for all. What she did receive was more of a slap in the face. "Why would you write that? Do you want to get your grandfather in trouble?" Done, and done; door slammed again in her face. Fuck you. I personally think she should have yelled at her mom until she was blue in the face, but this wasn't the first time this was brought up, and it wasn't the last time she would be let down.

At her girlfriend's house, she disclosed what had happened to her. If I knew then what I know now, she probably wouldn't have tried her entire life to rectify what happened to her. I would have hoped she would have just screamed long and loud until she was listened to. I still do not know why to this day she continued to give up every single time. She and I both knew deep down though that the support would be few and far between. It wouldn't be until she met her first husband that some light was shined on her broken heart caused by those who shouldn't have hurt her in the first place; but for now, her girlfriend said she was sorry that happened to her. At that moment, her compassion from her friend was the most she had ever received.

In the eighth grade, my darling girl had two issues. She started her period, and she had a weak bladder. Her friends used to make her laugh so much, she had peed her pants several times. She did hide it rather well, or if she didn't hide it, no one really picked on her. She was part of the popular group, which wasn't hard, but still. It was nice for her. Then there was one day at school when she had a pain in her stomach. It wasn't that bad, just uncomfortable. She went to the bathroom; she knew she wasn't dying, but still, she knew what happened. When she told her mom that she started her period, she wrote her a note. She didn't feel comfortable talking to her mom about this.

All her other friends could talk to their mothers. I know she was confused with why she couldn't. Her mom seemed to be excited for her. Why? She was bleeding from her vagina. That was disgusting. To this day, I know she hates sometimes the parts of being a female. I think it stems from her grandfather groping her lady parts. I don't think it helped either that the lines of communication were not very open. The safe sex talk went as this: *You get pregnant, we will put the baby up for adoption*. I was thinking, why did they not teach her how to not get pregnant. That would save her a lot of heartache later.

While becoming a "woman," she also spent her eighth grade year playing volleyball and basketball and running cross-country. All these sports were mandatory. I watched her grow, and while she didn't start out very good, she ended up playing rather well. Her favorite sport played that year was basketball. She would get lost in the counting of each basket she made during practice at home. She and her dad would play for hours. He pushed her and wouldn't let her quit. Their team came in second place, which was okay. She enjoyed learning the sport and had a lot of fun. She gained a lot of self-esteem. The school was very active, on the playground and as well as with extracurricular activities. The class went on a trip to Astro Camp, as well as church retreats with the youth group. She dove right into wanting to be a part of it all. She went on all the Bible retreats, trying to fit in. I know she wanted to be good but also wanted to be liked.

Her class had some very cute boys. She, of course, couldn't keep her hormones under control, and she was determined to get a boyfriend. I wouldn't say she was the ugly duckling in the group, but looking back, I was surprised she was able to get a boyfriend at all. I would say she was more of the matchmaker. She was even in the room with her friend while her friend and her boyfriend kissed for the first time. She, of course, had her eyes closed the entire time. Though she peeked. And I know she didn't like what she saw, because I know she liked this boy as well; however, she liked her friend, and she was happy her friend was happy. That was who she was. She always put others ahead of herself. For her, these trips were therapeutic; she was normal. I know she was trying to forget what had happened to her and the fact that her mom wasn't supportive.

The absurd thing was they did go to church every Sunday, so as a Christian family, wouldn't her mom know this was wrong? Her mom wanted her to be involved with her youth group, which she didn't mind. Both had different reasons for being so active. Deep down, I feel her mom wanted her to stay involved to try and pray the sin, which she didn't commit, away. On one of the Bible retreats, I remember her mom gave her twenty dollars for the weekend to buy food. Two days, six meals. The twenty dollars went fast. I watched her attempt to budget, but her youth leader caught on and was nice enough to feed her. She was embarrassed. Her mom did apologize for not giving her enough money, but shouldn't a parent know? Maybe she was just being a stubborn teenager who was being greedy? I know she was always afraid to say what her needs and wants were since her needs just a few years prior were ignored. I can honestly see she was confused on what to do, so she just kept pushing on. The more she pushed, the stronger she became. Nothing would break her.

During her eighth grade year, a boy liked her. She liked him as well, but there was something that kept her from saying yes to him when he would ask her out. Even though her class wasn't that big, I know she still wanted to be popular. She ended up "going out" with the popular guy. He was a joke. He was pasty white and not good-looking at all. He used to tease the guy who liked her, and she fell for it. Let me explain. "Going out" in the eighth grade was her and her friends going to the cheap theater in their hometown and seeing the same kids and watching the same movie a few times so that they can make out. She had her first official kiss during the movies. Kissing wasn't all that it was cracked out to be. Since she came from a public school, I know that people had their eyes on her. I felt at times she was the "bad" girl; however, she never did anything bad. She was boy-crazy, which was true, but I know she didn't go as far as people thought. She was more talk than anything. I think for her, she associated love with physical touch. I know she was also very confused because I know the touch she received from her grandfather wasn't appropriate, so when someone would attempt to kiss her, she felt awkward.

During winter recess of that year, her dad took her and her brother on a trip to visit her aunt and cousins. They were to be spending a week in the snow. I know she hadn't seen her cousins in years and frankly forgot what they looked like. When they arrived at the airport, I know her teenage hormones were going crazy. She saw this tall blonde-haired guy and for a moment had a fantasy about "what if." The tall blonde-haired guy came up to her a few moments later and introduced himself as her cousin. I know that me laughing in the corner wouldn't go over well if she could see me. I could see on her face. *Why does this always happen to me?* Even though she and her cousin didn't have any relation as far as blood goes, it was still weird that she had a two-and-a-half-second crush on him. But after that week, they became and—still are—close. During the trip, they skied all week. I know she had the greatest time. The one bad thing was that she was on her period. I know she felt so dirty and gross. She couldn't tell her two aunts that she was on her period and literally bled through all her clothes. I think this went back to her not being able to tell anyone anything. The week overall went well, and she was ready to get back to school. She was ready to finish the eighth grade and begin high school. For the rest of the school year, I know she did have a great time for the most part. They were a close knit group, and for once, she felt as though she belonged.

Her eighth grade class was a graduating class of four. It was a short and sweet ceremony. I know she wanted to believe that her life was going to change for the better. She made some great friends, and even though she ended up with the boyfriend who she didn't really want, it wasn't that bad. I know she had more good memories than not so good.

The summer before her freshman year, she attempted to try out for the volleyball team. She then realized she was leaving for vacation with her dad. Tryouts were never finished. I know she should have stuck with it. She was okay. While she was on vacation, her step-dad signed her up for all her classes. When freshman year started, she had a hope inside. She felt that she would be okay and that if she just focused on schooling, she would do fine. No boys. She was focused on becoming a teacher. She and I both knew that she was smart; however, she needed to focus more than others in her grade. She began to resent those whom school became easy to. I watched her put in the effort, but it wasn't good enough. Her first progress report was mostly Fs and Ds. I know she attempted to hide it from her mom, but it didn't work. She was now destined to bring home weekly progress reports to make sure she was turning in homework and participating in class. She would forge her teacher's signatures. Always. When she did get her report cards, she brought most of her grades up.

Since she brought her grades up, she could go on vacation with the family. They went to the Cayman Islands. This vacation was with her mom, stepdad, brother, her mom's older sister, cousin, and her uncle. She had the most amazing time on vacation. She could swim with sharks—non-threatening ones, but still, swimming with sharks was cool. The family took a tour over to a sandbar, where there were what seemed like hundreds of stingrays; they wrapped themselves around her. She was in heaven.

During the stay, she ran into a local. Well, he pretended to "trip" over her feet. He was good-looking, and apparently, he thought she was too. They exchanged addresses, and they were pen pals for a while after she made it back home. Nothing happened while they were on the islands, and while she was excited to meet this boy who liked the American girls, as an adult, I know she is relieved she didn't do anything with him. I have a feeling she would have ended up on the Missing Persons poster. Like I said, she never really did anything "bad girl"–like. She always thought about it; however, her conscience always got the best of her.

The worst part of the trip was her uncle. He was her mom's brother-in-law. Her uncle was, in so many words, a pervert. He would stare at her breasts, which unfortunately developed in the fifth grade. He made her uncomfortable. She didn't like to be alone with him. Nothing ever happened, and she wanted to be sure nothing ever did.

While on the island, she wanted to prepare for her sophomore year; she wanted to have her hair done in braids. Since her mom and stepdad worked for the airlines, she wasn't allowed to have her entire hair braided, but she was allowed a few on each side where she could hide them. She also bought a Bob Marley shirt. Her mom didn't really like the fact she wanted to wear a shirt with a guy who was dead and a drug addict. This was her mom's issue. I really think that her mom felt clothing and music were gateways to harder music and clothing—you know, thong panties. I know she wanted to find herself, yet she couldn't.

During her sophomore year, she used school as a social network for trying to find a boyfriend and be popular. Let's face it, she will never be popular. High school was such a blur. She never got a boyfriend even though her friend from junior high wanted to be her boyfriend. She couldn't ever say yes. She did say yes for a second, and then broke his high school heart because she really didn't like him that way. It wasn't him. It was her. She was damaged. She had a few crushes in high school. Some, when I think about it, I don't really understand why—except that they were cute. But then again, I was never a teenage girl. Thank god.

She hated high school. She despised it to the point that now as an adult, I know she remembers names and facts, just not times. I guess that is a good thing; and growing up, and in the grand scheme of things, high school was so insignificant. I do know she remembers one incident. Just one. When she became pregnant. While life happened for her so fast, I know this was the point where she attempted to better herself and, in turn, fucked her life good.

She had a crush on this guy, and one thing led to another. She was that girl who lost her virginity and became pregnant at the same time. Awesome. When she became pregnant, she was scared. She didn't want to tell anyone. She couldn't tell her mom, because when she was molested, her mom didn't want to believe her, and that wasn't even her fault. Now she chose to have unprotected sex and got pregnant. She did confide in a friend, and she told the father. The father was just as scared as she was, and his response wasn't very comforting.

The one girlfriend she told she was pregnant held her secret and well. She at first drove her to the clinic to see about an abortion. I guess by the time she asked for one, it was too late. Maybe that was God's way of telling her she was meant to have the baby. She ate well and exercised and took vitamins. She was on the track team and ran two miles a day. She was determined to hide this baby. She didn't have normal checkups because she didn't tell anyone. She tried her hardest to keep this secret. The thing with secrets, they always come out!

It was summer. I saw that she let her stomach relax, and her mom asked her if she was pregnant, because her stomach was big and hard. I heard her tell her no, and if she didn't believe her then, she should get her a test. Backfired again. Inside, I know she was hoping that her mom would say *Okay, let's go get a test*. She didn't. She believed her. She couldn't talk to her mom and let her know what happened. She didn't deserve her trust. I wish she had told at least her dad. Her dad would have been disappointed but would have helped.

She started her senior year, and it was getting harder to hide her belly. She wore her friend's football sweatshirt. She stole it from him for a long time. But she wore it, with the one pair of jeans that fit. It was hot; however, she didn't care. She needed to hide her stomach.

No one at school except her friend knew she was pregnant, and the dad thought she had an abortion because that was what he told her to do. I know she wasn't mad at him for suggesting it. They were both in high school. I know she never thought she would be a teenage mom. But again, her life is nothing how she thought it would be.

In October, after school one day, her stepdad was making fun of her because she was waddling when she walked. She had no idea that when you were pregnant and began the process of labor, your walk became even more noticeable. I guess all the walking and gravity helped. She went to her dad's for dinner. She didn't feel well. They had Mexican food that night. She loves Mexican food. Before they left the house, her water broke. Again, she didn't know what that was. She was wearing overalls, and you couldn't really tell she was wet. It was time to go home, and she made sure she sat on the edge of the seat so as to not get the seat wet in her dad's truck. They made it back home, and she went straight to her room to change her clothes. She vomited. Since she was in labor, it wasn't a good idea to eat anything. Her mom said she could stay home the next day, thinking she had the flu. She rarely stayed home. There was always so much going on that she didn't want to miss at school. She went to bed and began to have these shooting, rolling pains in her stomach. It was almost like a roller coaster was riding up and down on her stomach. This went on until the middle of the night. She changed her clothes several times. Finally, she couldn't take it anymore, and she went into the bathroom. She sat on the toilet thinking it was a bad stomachache. I watched her begin to push, and something told her to stand up. She stood up and felt in between her legs. There was a head. *Shit*! Her secret is going to come out! *Now*! She ended up pushing the baby out. She held on to the baby and then sat back down.

The baby began to cry. She tried to keep the baby from crying because she didn't want anyone to hear it. Wait, crying was good. She started to scream for her mom. Her mom didn't come in. Her stepdad had heard her and opened the bathroom door, then shut it quickly. As I was watching over her, I then heard screaming. "You were pregnant! Oh, my god!"

*Of course, Mom, let's scream at her while she is crying and holding a baby.* So supportive. Her stepdad called 911. They finally arrived in what seemed like forever. She was placed on the gurney. I know her teenage brain was thinking *Oh wow, cute guys, bad timing*. Her friend's parents, whom she has known since grade school, came over to see if everyone was okay. They saw the lights of the ambulance. It was a quiet neighborhood, nothing bad happened.

When her friend's parents came over, they immediately thought that her mom or stepdad had a heart attack or something was medically wrong. Their entire world was turned as well. I know the thoughts in people's heads. *She was pregnant?*

On the way to the hospital, her mom came with her. I heard her tell her mom that she loved her because she did; however, she was scared. I know she was so frightened that she would be in trouble. Little did she know that fifteen years later, the love of her life whom she had just given birth to would break her heart on a level that she didn't know existed. However, for now, she knew that all she could do was to be a great mom and do whatever it took to graduate high school. With a baby.

While she was in the hospital, her dad came to visit. He brought her roses. Pink. He's the only reason she even like roses. I heard her say that she thought they were an ugly flower. Her mom and stepdad did what they could in attempting to get nine months of preparation done in her room within a few days before she came home, with a baby. A baby. What did she do? She did give birth to a beautiful baby boy.

She decided right there that she would be the best mom, and because she was so young, their relationship would be amazing. She signed out of the traditional high school and started on the path of home school. She was still a part of the high school but collected her assignments from the continuation school. She also tried looking for a job. She needed to work. She was a mom. Her son was born in October. By Thanksgiving, she was working. She would take her son to daycare/nanny and would go to work. She would do her home-work and take care of her son. Repeat. She didn't realize how much of a challenge it would be to be a young mom. She didn't plan her pregnancy, but she honestly wasn't thinking when she had sex. All she knew was a boy liked her, and they went too far.

During the days before she got a job, her mom stayed at home with her to help her raise her son. She had asked her if she was raped. I saw it in her face, she wanted to scream at her. So she believed that someone would rape her, but it's impossible for someone who is her family to touch her inappropriately? Of course, she didn't say any-thing. I do remember a social worker coming to visit the house. How can a teenager hide her pregnancy? What kind of family was this? So many opportunities to spill the truth, but she couldn't, and to be honest, I don't blame her at all. Her family was no help, except when it was expected. Put on a good show.

During that first year, a lot happened. I remember her sitting on the couch when Columbine was shot up. I remember the girl who threw her baby in the trash at prom. All I kept thinking was, I know she will be the best mom and I know she won't let any harm come to her son. How can anyone harm a child?

When June came around, she was excited. She had gone to school and picked up her diploma. She did it. She was a high school graduate and all, with a baby and working. She brought her diploma out for her mom to see. She was hoping she would want to celebrate. Her mom had a disappointed look on her face. It crushed her. Her mom told her how she took the act of watching her graduate away from her. Wow. So, she did something people said she wouldn't be able to, and she was angry because she didn't wear a stupid gown and walk down an aisle with people whom she wouldn't really see anymore? Thanks. Asshole. I know she realized that from this moment, she would have to try and do things on her own.

She continued to work while she lived at home. She had the opportunity to move out with some friends, which backfired. She should have tried harder to move out. She didn't realize living at home would be a crutch. Not that her parents didn't help, because they did. She took advantage of the fact that they were around. She was an asshole at times. I don't think she meant it; it was more of an "I am trying to be an adult and don't know which way to go."

She was sad and lonely. Her friends were traveling and going to school. While I know she made the right decision to take care of responsibilities, I wonder what would have happened if she didn't. I wonder what would have happened if she gave her son up for adoption. The thought makes me sick; and I know if she could see me, I would get punched, right in the vagina. If I had one. I know her thought would be that she would be putting him in the same situation she was. He didn't ask to be here, and he didn't ask for this life, but now he must figure it out? She wasn't going to do that to her son.

While she was at her job, she met some interesting people. She worked in customer service. I know she enjoyed meeting different people every day, and she even enjoyed her coworkers. I thought she would make a career out of her job. She then had a bright idea. She would go back to school. She decided she would go to beauty school, because that was the in thing. Little did she know that there wasn't a creative bone in her body, at least when it came to beauty. She couldn't cut hair or paint nails to save her life. Let's face it. She was on her way to becoming a beauty school dropout. During the time, she put effort in trying a new career; I watched her continue to work the 9-5 job as well as take care of her son with the help of her family.

While she worked in customer service, I felt that she had somewhat of a life. She needed a life. Her parents helped her with the care of her son if she wanted to go out. She didn't go out much, if hardly ever. She was a part of the bowling team for work, which was fun for a little while. Since her social life was nonexistent, I watched her try online dating. She found most guys at that time just wanted sex, which wasn't fun for me at all to witness. I was watching this little girl grow up, and she wasn't little anymore. For her, I know she wasn't looking for just sex, but sometimes that happened. I remember this one guy came over, and they hung out. Since she still lived at home, she had to be careful of who she brought over. He was a firefighter. The strange thing was when he came over, he looked like he had done meth. His teeth were so gross. He was nice enough, so they hung out. Don't ask me why, but they had sex. I don't even know why they did.

The real shitty thing was when she went to work later that day, she got a phone call. From her dad. He knew her department, and he knew she would answer calls. As soon as she answered the call, he told her to speak calmly and softly but pretty much telling her how much trouble she was in because the douchebag had left his condom stuffed in her mom's couch. *Ugh.* She finished her shift and went to her dad's house. He was watching her son while she was at work. Her dad slapped her across the face. Her dad never put hands on her. As soon as he did it, he felt bad. I know she didn't care. She left the house, and he watched her son that night. She went to a party that she initially wasn't going to go to and hung out with her coworkers. She felt miserable. I know she was confused, and she didn't know where her life was going and what she was doing. Part of her felt as though this was what she can be doing because of her age, and then her conscious knew she needed to be home with her son. To be honest, I think she was feeling as though she was starting to spin out of control. She wasn't into doing drugs or drinking a lot, but this night she did drink. From the combination of booze and lack of sleep, she shouldn't have driven home, but she did. She was only a few miles away. She arrived home early in the morning. She fell asleep on the couch. She awoke to a hard thump on her head. She awoke to her son who could barely walk, holding a handheld massager; it left a nice bump. I always felt it was her mom who hit her on the head and then had her son hold it so when she woke up, she would see her son and think that he was the one who was mad and hit her. Little did she know it was her son; however, she wouldn't know that until many years later. Some would think this incident was a child being just that, but her son had always lashed out with anger at his mom, even at the youngest of ages. She just never wanted to admit there was a problem.

From the time she had her son until the time she met her ex-husband, the timeline is a blur. I remember events, but not exactly when it happened. I think a part of me wants to forget certain memories; however, God wants me to remember. I don't know if this is part of the guardian angel guidelines. We remember the events for those who we are protecting. These memories are who she is, so I know she remembers as well, even if they are shoved in her subconscious.

While working in the grocery store, she began a friendship with a girl the same age as herself. They both had sons who were the same age. I am unsure of how their friendship formed. At that age and being young moms, they were toxic together; but her mom liked to blame her friend for everything that happened. The more her mom blamed her, the more of a rebel my sweet girl became.

She continued the online dating and met someone who was in the Marine Corps. She had never dated anyone from the Marines, and she figured, what could go wrong? They had a pretty good relationship going. He was from New York, and he was respectful to her family. He was a ginger. She hated gingers. He spent the holidays with them, and things were going well. One night while she was home, and he was on base, she went to call him from the directory on base, and another guy answered. She thought this new guy was joking with her, but then later she found out her boyfriend and the guy on the other end of the phone had the same last name, and in fact, her boyfriend's extension was one number off. Because of her mistake, she started talking to this new guy, and they became friends. She didn't tell her boyfriend about her new friend because we know how guys get, and even though nothing was going on, she didn't want him to get jealous.

I do remember in February that she wanted to wish her best friend from childhood a happy birthday. This was the guy who she never said yes to when he would ask her out in high school. She always loved him, just never like that. Her boyfriend had spent the night at her house, and when she got off the phone with her best friend, she was interrogated by him on who she was talking to. I remember she tried explaining who it was, but then she became angry with him. How dare he question her on who she was talking to? Her boyfriend expressed that he wanted to hit her because she shouldn't talk to him like that and she needed to tell him who she was talking to. At that moment, I remember she became angry, and she told him to get the fuck out of her house and that she didn't want to see him again. In a normal place of residence, if anyone were to leave, they can get in their car or walk down the street to the bus.

I am laughing now because when she told him to get the fuck out, there was nowhere he could go. It took twelve to fifteen minutes to drive from her house to town. To the next city, it is about a thirty-minute drive. It was raining, and her stupid bleeding heart gave him a ride down the hill to the mall where he could catch the bus. As she was about to drive off into the rainy day, he asked her if she had any money for the bus. Seriously? You want to hit her, and now you are asking her for money? She gave him the last five dollars she had, and she never saw him again. She went home and called her friend. The one with the same last name as her now ex-boyfriend. I personally think she should have toned it down with the guys, but she was only eighteen, and this is what eighteen-year-olds do. Luckily, she never had sex with her now ex-boyfriend. Like I said, she hated gingers.

She continued to work and go to school, but then her mom and stepdad noticed a behavior change. To her, she thought she was doing just fine, juggling everything. She wasn't.

Before her life went completely out of control, her mom and stepdad went to see an attorney—without her, of course. They wanted to see their options of helping with their grandson. Personally, I think they were a little salty from not being allowed to adopt him. They offered, but she wanted to do the right thing and take responsibility for her actions. This is how things unfolded. I know she should have said no, but she felt as though she owed her parents.

It all started with her mom asking if they could have temporary guardianship so that way, she could grow up and live a little. She agreed because she did need the help; however, she didn't realize when she wanted her son back how difficult it would be to jump through the hoops. It started out that she would go through the motions—work, school, home, be a mom 24/7. She never wanted to ask for a break, but her mom did say that she could go out if she wanted. The reason for the guardianship was just that. For her to have a bit of a life, and if something happened to her, her son would be covered legally by her parents. For her, it was really confusing, because she wanted to do the right thing by her son; however she wanted to be a kid. She didn't realize that being a kid was over, even with the help of her parents.

I watched as she and her girlfriend started slowly to be out till all hours of the night. The freedom bug had hit her. Something snapped. They didn't do anything that would be considered "wrong" or "illegal." There were no drugs or drinking. They just never wanted to go home. Her friend always stayed with her. The longer they were out, the easier it was for her not to go home. Her friend's mom had no issue watching her son with no consequences. There were times when she wouldn't go home and go straight to cosmetology school the next day. I watched her mom show up and ask her if she would go home. I know she was so angry with her. All her past was surfacing. Why should she go home? What was there? Her son was there. She just couldn't. She wanted to figure out who she was as a person. She had been told since she was little what type of person she was to be and how she should behave. I personally believe she wanted to explore some options. She wasn't a bad person, just young.

After a few weeks of working and school, during this temporary guardianship thing, she decided she wanted to meet her Marine friend. The friend she had been speaking to on the phone. They had yet to meet in person.

One night, she and her friend went to meet her guy friend in person. He lived on base, and I know she was nervous to meet him in person. She really liked him and hoped he liked her as well. When they finally met up, and she met this guy, I know she thought he was the cutest guy she had ever met. He was sweet and polite as well. He was from the Midwest. They eventually hung out a few times, and then they were going to have an official date. They ended up drinking that night and having a good time with her girlfriend and his roommate. This night, she did have sex with this guy. Then for some stupid reason, she had sex with his roommate.

Little did she know, she was set up. They wanted to get her drunk to see if she would "cheat" on this guy. They weren't a couple yet, but this was the preliminary test. Apparently, he was used to girls treating him poorly, and this was a test. It was a pretty fucked-up test, and she lost. For the longest time, I know she thought she was the asshole, but she realized that if you get a girl drunk and set her up, you are the asshole. I am not saying she wasn't wrong, but to set anyone up is a dick move. After that, she cooled it with the guys. She saw him months later sitting at a bus stop, looking as cute as ever. She gave him a ride home; that was it. She never saw him again.

One night, she and her girl were out after they got off work. They were driving around looking for things to do. They ended up meeting another Marine. They hung out with him and his friend. They didn't do anything with them sexually; she really was just done with guys. She did know she should spend more time at home, but she did like her freedom. She didn't realize her freedom would screw her royally. At this point, she didn't care, even though her heart ached for her son, and she knew she was now a bad mother.

While I was watching her screw up her life, I couldn't say shit. I think now she would have punched me if she found out I was watching out for her. I was horrible at this. To be honest, I think I was only around so she wouldn't die. In the span of just a few months, she fucked herself good. These mistakes were fixable, but man, she was on a good one.

She dropped out of beauty school, and for some reason, she quit her really good job. What was she doing? She was also alienating herself more from the family. She didn't care; her heart was broken.

During this time of rebelling against her family, she found herself hanging out with more military guys. She went out on a few dates, which didn't end up anywhere—except she did get to sit in a fighter jet. I thought she was going to have an orgasm doing so. She loves jets till this day. I don't know what happened to that guy; he was nice and didn't try anything funny. I honestly believe she felt as though she was shit, and she deserved shit.

She and her girlfriend went on a double date with a guy her friend had been seeing. The other guy in the mix wasn't the initial date but a substitute. I wish I could have told her to run, but her self-esteem had plummeted, so she just turned off all feelings.

They didn't have much in common other than a physical attraction. She knew he was a piece of shit, but at the same time, the bad boy allure appealed to her. He started having rules for her. He hated when she would speak to other guys, and she wasn't allowed to be friends with anyone from her past. Her dad didn't like him, which should have been the biggest clue.

All they did was go out to eat, go to the movies, and have sex all the time. Every time they had sex, it was consensual, and yet it was meaningless. Then after a fight they had, he wanted to have sex, and she didn't. You don't tell him no. He raped her. He was mean and held her down, and she continued to tell him *no*. They have had rough sex before, so when she tried telling someone about it, they thought she was full of shit; but her gut wasn't having it. She knew it was wrong. She was a very physical being, but she knew what she wanted and what she didn't. This was one of the greatest things about her.

She however was dating a Marine. It was like a boy's club. No one wanted to help her. So she was shit out of luck.

She found out after that incident that she was pregnant. Awesome, now she was going to be labeled a slut. The thing with her was she didn't give a shit how many people you have slept with, as far as being a male or female. Some people just like sex. She liked it, but she didn't like it when she was taken advantage of. She knew the line, and the pieces of shit who crossed it deserve to die.

After the incident, she cut herself off from him completely. She decided to focus on finding a new job while being pregnant. Fuck. This was going to be awesome. She hid her pregnancy for as long as she could. Sound familiar?

She was scared shitless. She tried hiding it, but her dad found out that she was pregnant. She was living at her dad's house when this happened. Her mom and stepdad kicked her out a few weeks prior. They felt she wasn't a good influence on her son and wanted her out. So she moved, two blocks away. When her dad found out about the pregnancy, he was so disappointed in her. She knew he was upset when he didn't wish her a happy birthday that year. This was her dad. He was her shining star. She was his little girl, and he just couldn't look at her. I know her mom thought she did this on purpose. It was decided that she would put the baby up for adoption. She didn't believe in abortion. She is pro-choice, but for herself, she didn't believe in termination.

She was dropped off to stay with her aunt and uncle while going through this adoption process. The adoption agency was in Orange County. Her aunt and uncle were amazing people who took her in, and they worked through what was needed. Her aunt had made an appointment to go see a birth counselor. She did the intake, and then she could look through pictures of families. There were some who had children already but always looking for more, and then there were couples waiting. I noticed she was being pressured into picking a family that already had children. The vibe she got was to look for another couple. As she was looking through the books, she noticed a couple who very well could be related to her. She decided to meet this couple. I know she wanted her child to be with a loving family. She also met with a couple whom no one had met with yet. They looked kind and were well off. This couple in the picture looked just like her. This was a bonus for when the baby would be born.

I remember her doing her hair and painting her toes. She put on a pair of beige overalls and a pink tank top. She looked cute. I know she was so nervous about meeting this family. Just a husband

and wife. She found out that the wife could get pregnant, but if she did, her health would fail, and she could die. To her, that was just as bad as not being able to conceive. She began to tell the couple her story. She cried badly, but of course, they didn't judge her. I know she felt safe talking to them. They were the only couple she met. They connected, and I know she fell in love. This family could provide for this baby.

After meeting with the family, she went back home until the time she would give birth.

Until the time she gave birth, she stayed inside a lot. No one was to know of this awful secret. She was to stay away from all the family. She tried to spend time with her son, supervised of course. She apparently was a danger to herself and her son. One day, she did spend the day with her mom and son. I am unsure of what they were doing, but I do know that she told her mom she didn't want her to meet the family she was putting her baby up for adoption to. Something inside her screamed that she didn't want her mom involved. My sweet girls mom told her that it was her "right" to be there when my girl gave birth.

I know she loved her mom, but her mom hurt her badly. She couldn't get over it. She had her aunt and her dad's girlfriend, and she was okay. As they were driving back from the outing, her mom began to yell and scream at her while her son cried in the back seat. Her mom was speeding down the winding road to their house. She yelled, "Why don't I just fucking kill us all." I thought she was going to kill them; it was painful to watch. She swerved their truck to head toward the embankment. Fortunately, someone was watching out for them, and they didn't crash. All because she didn't want her mom there while she gave birth. What a psycho.

The moment they arrived at the house, she went to take her son out of the back seat. Her mom grabbed him out of her arms and said that he was hers and to get the fuck away from the house.

She walked back to her dad's house. She cried all the way there. While they only lived a few blocks from each other, it seemed to take a long time to walk. I don't know if it was because she was pregnant or emotional. It could be both.

Until the time she gave birth, she did nothing but stay up all night watching movies in her room and sleep all day. Her dad worked. She had no friends and rarely went outside. She kept to herself. She didn't even talk to her friend. The girl who she spent all that time with messing around. She spoke on the phone to the adoptive parents all the time. She also had to get the rights signed away by the douchebag, and she also needed to get some of her belongings back from him. He had her stereo. I forgot why she allowed him to borrow it, but she did. Her dad refused to drive her to get it. She had to take the bus, to base from her house. It was a long trip.

She arrived on base to see the guy who raped her. Her family still didn't know. I know she just didn't want to disappoint them anymore, and for her not to do that, she needed to be an adult. Growing up the way she did, there were expectations, and she failed every step of the way. So admitting that she was raped would be another disappointment. Her family would have accused her of putting herself in that situation in the first place. Yet as a child, she didn't put herself in any situation, and that happened. I know she spoke with the douchebag and spoke to him about signing his rights away. He even gave her a ride home. That was the last time she ever saw him. Except for social media, she hasn't seen him in person. She likes to keep tabs on him to make sure he never ventures back to California. He was quick to sign his rights away. From that moment, I know she thought her life and world would be looking up. For a while it was.

In November, while big and pregnant, she began to talk to this guy she found on Love AOL. She was bored and was sick of being lonely. He seemed nice, but he was a Marine. Another one? She couldn't possibly date another Marine. She then realized that not all guys are the same and not all Marines are the same. They spoke on the phone for about two weeks, and they e-mailed. She told him her situation. He became angry and judgmental of her. She should have stopped talking to him right then and there, but she felt he was right. They planned to meet and go to the movies. He picked her up on December 1. From that moment, they were always together. Even with her being pregnant, he was there for her. There were many red flags, but she ignored them. He would even yell at her if she gave him the wrong directions, something that was uncalled for.

There were many reasons why she should have stopped dating him, but she ended up falling for him. They would go on picnics and spend the entire night up until the sun rose. Her dad allowed him to stay at their house if he slept in the living room. She was fine with that. And just like that, they were a couple. Young and stupid. Right after Christmas, she was to stay up in Orange County until the baby was born. She was staying with her birth counselor. The birth counselor was someone the adoption agency set up to take to appointments and to talk about life and shit. She was okay, but I knew this would be a short-lived relationship. She was invited to stay with her birth counselor after the baby was born to get on her feet and start anew. She decided to take her up on it. She would be out of her hometown and, literally, can start over. Her first goal after she gave birth was to get her son back.

The day of the birth, her aunt would be in the delivery room with her, and I know her mom was upset because she wouldn't let her in the room with her. Her aunt didn't judge her. She never did. She never will.

They arrived at the hospital, and she was induced. It was a tough labor. She was in a lot of pain. The baby was coming "sunny side up." Babies come face down. Not this sucker; he wanted to be faced up, and that hurt. The baby was born healthy. She didn't hold this beautiful child for fear that she would change her mind. Even though the circumstances weren't normal, this baby was part of her; but she knew better. She was taken to her room to recuperate. Her mom did show up and stayed with her in her room after the baby was born. Her boyfriend also came and officially met her mom. It was rather awkward. People asked her why she allowed her mom to stay but not allow her in the delivery room. Part of her still needed her mom, and this was that time. She knew she would get her needs met, and the company was nice.

It was the day of her discharge. I know she wanted to say bye to the baby's parents and say bye to the wonderful gift she could provide. She didn't hold the baby, but she did look and say a quick prayer that they would have a wonderful life. Her boyfriend stood with her while she said goodbye. That meant a lot.

As she left the hospital, she was hoping to leave a horrible past behind and was looking forward onto a bright future.

Just a week later she married her boyfriend. What was she thinking? They had only dated for a month.

They attempted to hide the marriage from her family. They, however, couldn't. Her mom was suspicious and went to do some digging in public records. They were going to have a ceremony later but wanted to get married. Her husband wanted to take care of her with benefits and help her start a new life. They lived with her birth counselor in her condo. She got a job with a grocery store, and he was not that far from her on base. Things were rather tight with her birth counselor, and while she did appreciate the help, it was time to move on. She and her husband found an apartment closer to her family and her son, and she quit the grocery store. She wanted to focus on school. They lived in an awful neighborhood, but it was their first place. He would work, and she did the school thing.

Then her country, her beautiful home was attacked. Since she was a Military wife, she was super freaked because she couldn't reach her husband. She ended up driving up to her mom's house. She was in shock. How could anyone do that? Being a spouse in the military, there were a lot of conversations normal families didn't have. They would go back and forth on whether he was to go overseas. It was nerve-wracking. They just carried on and did what they needed to do.

One weekend while they were at her parents' house, she woke up and found out that her face was a little numb. She went to the bathroom and washed her face and brushed her teeth. She attempted to smile, and it was crooked. She was mortified. The term of what was happening was Bell's palsy. From this moment, she would continue to struggle with a few cases of Bell's palsy and eventually lead to nerve damage. Communicating and keeping her eyes from staying open was the worst of it. Within a few months, her face went back to normal, except for her crooked smile.

Besides the Bell's palsy, her life was looking up. She was in the process of getting her son back. It was a hard and long road, but she jumped through all the hoops. Her husband wasn't to leave for overseas just yet. They were accepted to live on base, and that's when the hoops were over. While her parents were disappointed in the fact that she got married without telling anyone, they were getting used to the idea and realized that maybe this was a good fit. I know she was a proud Marine wife. She felt she had a good life living on base. While living on base, her son was adopted by her husband. It was a very happy day in the family. Her son's biological father was never in the picture, and even though the door was open, her son needed a dad. She didn't realize the impact of what was going on with her son once he was adopted. There are some days now when she regrets the decision. One doesn't know what is coming, and you can only do so much at that time.

Both she and her husband settled into a routine of her being a housewife and him going to work. She did go to the local community college. She still wanted to be a teacher. She loved school. She also loved being a wife and mother. Her life was looking up. I kept wondering if her life was looking up, why I was still watching out for her.

In November, she found out she was pregnant. They were trying, but she was scared to have a baby because of all the trouble she had in the past. They announced their pregnancy on Thanksgiving. They spent Thanksgiving up with his family and called hers. Her family was very accepting because she was married now. I know she was hoping for a baby girl; she really wanted to have a daughter.

During her pregnancy, I know she spoke with her husband about baptizing the baby. He became extremely volatile and yelled at her that they would not be baptizing the baby because he didn't believe in God. He didn't care that she believed in God. She kept pushing the issue, and one, day he pinned her hands behind her back and shoved her into the arm rest of the couch. She in turn threw a Bible at him. I don't think throwing a Bible did any good, but it sure made her feel better. She stopped pressuring him about baptizing. I know she didn't want to have the chance of him hurting the baby.

Things calmed down, and she was back to being the loving wife. They had more good days than bad, and it wasn't as though her husband was a bad man. He had a temper and needed to control it. He was brought up in a household where yelling was common, and as I recall, her husband stated his dad would call him a "pussy" if he ever got hurt. The cycle of abuse comes in all forms. She didn't know how deep it went, and she was about to find out.

In December, they found out that her husband would be going overseas. They didn't know when exactly. Every day was a waiting game. She continued to go to school and focused on being a mom and wife. The day before the Super Bowl, her husband found out he was leaving for Iraq. She cried and then prepared to see him off. Her parents came to say bye and offered to stay with her that night. She said bye to her husband and then she went to bed. She had to get up early to take her son to preschool. She dropped him off and went home to cry. She was extremely emotional. Part of her wondered what would have happened if he never came home.

They would write letters, and she would send care packages. She even bought recorders to tape conversations while he was gone. She thought this would help not miss him so much, but she was wrong. She was miserable and was trying her best to be a good mom. I know she felt that she was failing. Her son was not happy, and he began to act out. He would sneak into her closet with a jar of peanut butter and eat the entire thing. She was unsure of why this behavior was happening and just attributed it to her husband being away. Her brother and her mom would help during the week while she went to school. Her mom would stay one day, and her brother would stay the other. One night, she and her brother went to get dinner. I watched as they attempted to put her son in the car to go get dinner, and he began to kick and hit her in the stomach. It took both of them to put her son in the back seat and buckle him in. I know she was at a loss and didn't know what to do anymore.

She had a friend down the street, and she thought if her son hung out with her daughter things would get better. It helped, but when he was at home, he was a terror. Her son was constantly ruining the carpet with food or whatever he could find; he wouldn't sleep or listen. The only time she got a break was when he was at school. Even on days when she would volunteer, he wouldn't listen to her; but he would listen to his teachers, so she figured just let it be.

She found out she was having a baby girl and was so overjoyed. She told her husband one day in a letter. She thought he would have been happy with either a boy or girl, but man, having a daddy's girl was the best news he had heard.

She was to be born in July, and I know she desperately wanted her husband to be there for the birth of their daughter. They were now in May, he was still gone, and her son was still acting like a terror.

During Mother's Day weekend, her parents took them to Arizona to stay at a resort. It was nice. They hung out by the pool all day. She needed to relax and just get away for a while. When they got home, she received a phone call that set her entire world upside down. She was part of the Military Key Wives. They are privy to information before others. She was called and was told that while her husband and his unit was in Kuwait waiting to go into Iraq, a land mine had gone off, and his CO was blown to pieces. He was still alive, but they were transporting him to another base. Her husband was okay. I know she was not okay and had to drive down the hill to go home. She misplaced her military ID, and when she got to base and they asked her for it, she completely lost it. She was pregnant and hormonal, and she began to sob right there in the middle of the ID checkpoint.

The MP had her pull over into guest parking and asked her some information about who she was and where she lived. She told him what housing she lived in and gave him her address. She showed him her license. He was so compassionate. He offered to drive her home, but she declined. She only had a mile to go. She would be okay for the rest of the drive. All she had to do was compose herself. It was hard being pregnant and with a little boy who just wouldn't quit. She was miserable. Her son blamed her for his daddy leaving. She had a hard time explaining that it wasn't her decision but that this was part of his dad's job. He thought his mom was shit. This wouldn't be the last time he vocalized his hatred for his mom.

Being a military wife during war time was extremely difficult. They had to deal with monsters who would do and say anything to hurt the military. While one doesn't agree with what the military does, to take it out on the families in inexcusable. I remember she was at a gas station and a lady decided to berate her because of the military sticker she had on the back of her car. My girl had a bat in the back seat, and all she wanted to do was bash her windows in for being so disrespectful. She then realized that her ignorance wouldn't change, especially with violence. She got in her car and left. She just wanted her husband to come home. There were nights she wondered what she would do if he never came home. To her this was a battle she had in her heart and her head. She knew that when he came home, the honeymoon would be over soon. Her husband was an angry man; even though she loved him deeply, he wouldn't change. She tried to be the good wife he wanted.

During the months her husband was gone, she kept herself busy. Her son was interviewed by the base newspaper. Her son told the reporter that his daddy had to go away because his boss (the president) needed his daddy to stop bad guys. This is what she told him when he asked why her husband left. It was the only thing she could say. She was also relieved he didn't tell the reporter it was his mommy's fault. She was so proud to see her son on the cover of the newspaper. I am sure her husband threw it away after they divorced years later.

While living on base, she made a few friends. She made three friends, and she keeps in touch with them still. She doesn't talk to them on a regular basis, but the one positive thing about social media is that she can locate them to say hello. One of her girlfriend's husbands was gone at the same time as her husband. Her husband was a piece of work. He was abusive to her, bad. I know my girl didn't think at the time her husband abused her because he never put her in the hospital, but later she learned that abuse is abuse.

Since her girlfriend was miserable with her husband while he was gone, she went on the prowl. She met a guy at a bar. He was a real nice Marine. I know she was unsure of the entire situation, but he apparently had a girlfriend or wife as well. Her girlfriend and her new Marine were seeing each other for a while and got a side apartment out in town. She was going to leave her husband. Or so she thought. As soon as her husband came home, she couldn't stand up to her husband and moved back in. I know my girl felt bad for her friend because she was genuinely a good person; she was just in a bad situation and felt she couldn't get out of it.

It was in June when she got the phone call, her husband would be coming home from war. She received the phone call from one of the other wives in the Key wife club. The phone tree had started. Then she received a phone call from a very irate Marine. On the other end was a man who was to respect the wives of the company and instead called her a stupid bitch because apparently, the information had changed when the unit would be arriving. The thing with deployments is times do change. What this asshat didn't realize was she was friends with the captain's wife. You don't mess with a wife of a Marine, and you don't mess with a pregnant wife of a Marine. This Marine was told by the captain to never speak to a wife or any woman that way ever again. When her husband finally arrived, she had found out the two of them had it out while in the desert, so he figured he would take his anger out on her. The homecoming was amazing. Lots of hugs and tears; their son forgot for a second how much he hated his mom. This next few weeks was to be nothing but rest and fun.

She had made plans with her friend down the street to have a BBQ and to catch up. Part of the reason to have the BBQ was to try and have things normal again and also to keep her friend's husband from being abusive. She had seen a little bit, but nothing was going to make her ready for what was about to happen.

The men got the BBQ started, and the women made the rest. Since she was pregnant, she wasn't drinking; however, the rest of them drank all night long. Her husband fell asleep on the couch, with their son upstairs in her friend's daughter's room. In the middle of the night, there was a loud banging, and then two people were coming downstairs in a heated argument. I know she pretended she was asleep until she couldn't anymore. Her husband slept throughout the entire ordeal. He was a selfish prick. Her friend's husband was angry that there was flirting going on. I know I didn't see the flirting, so I was wondering if it was the alcohol; and once again I must watch over my sweet girl and couldn't protect her. I think he was drunk and being a dick. I saw her continue to "sleep" until he pulled a knife on her friend. That was when she woke up and attempted to try and speak to him in a calm matter. This man had a knife, and she was ready to give birth the next month. So yes, it was a great idea to get in the middle. Why did she want to get in the middle, especially while being pregnant?

Her friend's husband told her that this was none of her fucking business and that he didn't care. He told her he would hurt her as well. I know she started to see *red*. She began to yell at him and told him that he wouldn't hurt her or her friend. She explained that their kids were upstairs. She tried to get him to put down the knife. He finally did; however, he grabbed her friend by her hair. He walked toward the front door and used her head to open it. She ran after them outside as he was beating the shit out of her, in the front yard, on a military base. As she was yelling, trying to get the beating to stop, she looked up, and there were people watching from the windows. She began to yell. "Listen, you nosy fucks! We need help." No help came. For the next ten minutes, her friend was being dragged by her hair in and out of the house, but this time, she held the door open for them so they could come in. She hated that her friend was being used to open the door with her head and then slammed into the door again in the opposite direction.

While the two of them were fighting all throughout the downstairs, she picked up the cordless phone. Her friend's husband caught her and threatened her to give up the phone. While she was being threatened, she also attempted to wake up her husband. No use, he was out for the count. Lightweight. The only thing she could think of was to run down the street. Have you ever seen an eight-month pregnant female run? It's not pretty. She rang the bell of her husband's staff sergeant's house. His wife answered and knew that there was trouble. No one comes calling at two in the morning unless there was an issue. She could get his staff sergeant to come down the street to dismantle the fight.

The cops, or the military police, were called, and both were separated. Her friend's husband returned the next day since her friend fought back. If she was just a "victim," he would have gone to jail; but since she defended herself, he got off. What the fuck was that all about? So you die, he goes to jail; you protect yourself, and he gets a slap on the wrist? Must love the military and how they protect their own.

The next week was rather silent. I know the baby shower for the beautiful baby girl was to happen; however her friend stated she couldn't host the baby shower anymore, due to her prick of a husband taking all her money. She did attend, which was fine; but her mother paid for the baby shower. Great, another thing to hold over her.

In July, her husband was to be discharged from the Marine Corps. They found an apartment a few cities away and prepared to move. They moved on a Friday, and that Monday, her baby girl was born. She may not have been born on the Fourth of July, however that little girl was a firecracker. She was her love.

She was born a few weeks early and came out brown. She had jaundice; fortunately, it cleared. They could leave the hospital in the normal time and begin life with a newborn.

Her husband was trying to adjust to being a civilian. She still went to school and stayed at home with her daughter, and their son was in school as well. They stayed in the apartment for about a year. She made a friend upstairs, whom she still talks to. Her friend didn't like her husband. She thought he was a tool and didn't like when she would hear them fight. They fought all the time. A few times, her friend would be protective and butt in, but then it got to the point of being pointless.

During that year, they bought their first home. It wasn't in San Diego. The home was in Riverside. This was further away from her family. She felt good about their decision though. Their first house before she hit the age of twenty-five. With everything in her past, she didn't think this would happen. She was determined to keep up the good momentum.

While living in their home, they had quite a year. They had a combined birthday and house-warming party for their daughter.

For once, she was excited to show off something she had accomplished. Her entire family was invited, as well as her husbands' who came down from Northern California. The guests started to arrive, and while she didn't like her grandmother or grandfather, they were invited. The moment her grandmother came to the house, she noticed a hole in the front yard. She stated, "How cute, a swimming pool." What a bitch.

The birthday party was overall a success, and their daughter even took her first steps. It was awesome.

After the party, I noticed my sweet girl start to have anxiety attacks for no reason. She and her husband seemed to be doing well, and she was in a rhythm of school and being a mom and wife. These anxiety attacks were caused every time her grandmother would call. It was getting to the point where the phone would ring, and she wouldn't answer because she knew who it was. This had to stop. Her husband was concerned and asked her how he could help. He knew of her past, and she told him that this had to stop. She was concerned that her daughter would be in danger if she were to be around her grandmother and grandfather.

I watched this man—who had a temper, who wasn't right for her at all—become human to the point where I thought for just a second, maybe he did care. I know he cared, he just wasn't soft. He called her parents and explained to her mom what was going on. Her mom spoke to the grandparents. Apparently, the talk went well. The grandparents wanted to talk to my sweet girl and talk it out. Finally, she thought! There will now be a healing process.

The time was all set. She was ready to drive down from Riverside to San Diego. Her phone rang, and it was the grandmother. Apparently, the grandmother was packing for a cruise and had to postpone the talk till they got back. The cruise was a two-week cruise. The grandmother decided that the health and well-being of their granddaughter wasn't important enough to spend an hour and talk to her. At that moment, my sweet girl cut ties from her grandparents, and apparently, that decision was her also cutting ties with the rest of the family. Like I said, her grandmother was law.

After this decision was made, I watched my sweet girl get back into the swing of things of being the best mom she could be.

That school year, their son was to be in the first grade. A week prior to school starting, they were at the park. They had ridden their bikes, and their son was playing on the monkey bars. I know she was nervous about him playing on the monkey bars, but her husband continued to push their son to cross. He didn't make it and fell. She heard the break from across the park. While they weren't far from their house, her husband went to the first house he could find to call 911. The ambulance showed up and took their son to the emergency room. Her husband went in the ambulance while she drove behind them in their car. I am not sure why she didn't go in the ambulance, but it didn't matter.

The break was clean, and a cast was put on. This was to be fun, starting school with a broken arm. It didn't really matter because their son and school had a hateful relationship, every single year. During parent-teacher conferences that year, the teacher explained to her that her son spoke out and goofed off. She thought it was boys being boys, little did she know he would be like this until he graduated high school.

They finished off the school year and ended up moving back down to San Diego. They found another place to buy. This time, it was a mobile home. While mobile homes have a stigma, this one wasn't so bad. They did own the property the mobile home was on, instead of renting. While they were waiting for the home to close, she and her husband, with kids in tow, moved back up to her mom's house to save money. They lived in her parent's garage. In the middle of summer. It was miserable, but it was free, so they made it work. When the house finally closed, they moved in slowly. There was a lot of work to be done. Besides doing summer session in school while he worked, she also painted the house. She loved to paint. It was therapeutic for her. While she painted, he ripped up the carpet and put in wood flooring. It was beautiful. Their house was coming together.

There were a lot of great things about living in the house and some negative as well. On either side of them were very different people. On the one side was a lady who had MS, and she stayed indoors all the time. The heat really bothered her in the summer. The other side of them was a lady who was a hermit. She never came out of her house unless it was to go to work. The house was always closed, and you can just tell it was dirty. Across the way was a family. The husband had a bad temper. Then there was the elderly couple who also lived across the street.

The elderly couple knew the neighborhood; it was their domain. They were the nicest couple, but don't mess with those they care about.

The temper man decided one day to yell at the neighbor with MS because he felt her dog was urinating on the lawn. It wasn't her dog, but he came irate. My sweet girl overheard him yelling and stepped in. My sweet girl allowed people to walk over her; however, when someone else was not able to help themselves, she would step in. Within a week, a "For Sale" sign was on the lawn.

One day, a family moved in. Very tall, beautiful family. This event in the neighborhood would start a friendship that is still going strong.

*****

Disclaimer. Before I go any further, I need to stop. I need to explain that the next part of her story is filled with violence and heartache. More than she has seen yet. This is when she completely broke down and her world was shattered. The most traumatizing part of this next piece is that there were only a few who were there to help her.

*****

There was something bubbling underneath the surface of her. She finished her first piece of schooling with a certificate for psychological and social services.

She was very proud of her accomplishment and was looking forward to the next step in her life. She could get an interview at a residential facility with at-risk youth. She didn't know that this life was going to be a part of her for the next decade.

As a celebration for her graduating, she and her husband made a trip to New Orleans. They had won tickets to the House of Blues to see a band. They won a meet-and-greet as well. Even though she wasn't a huge fan of this band, it was fun to go. They did sightseeing and ate a lot of amazing food, and the alcohol, the drinking did not stop the entire weekend.

The night before the show, my girl and her husband went out on the town. She had started out with two Hurricanes, the signature drink. She went on to having two beers and two shots of Jägermeister. It wasn't the amount of alcohol she had, it was the time frame in which she drank it. My girl loved to get lost in her booze.

Over the course of the night, they continued to drink and party. The two of them ended up at a bar with live music. My girl noticed a woman trying to get the attention of the band. She kept pulling up her shirt and was showing her bra. "Fuck this," my girl said! "This is how it's done." She walked right up to the band and lifted her shirt. She also had lifted her bra. They invited her on stage. My girl is so thankful social media wasn't huge back then. What a night.

Leaving to go back to the hotel and both extremely drunk, her husband started to walk in the wrong direction. She attempted to get him to follow her; he refused. Fuck this shit, she was out. As she walked down the streets in a city she didn't know, drunk as all hell, she knew she had to get to her room. She took off her wedding ring and put it in her pocket. She zipped up her hoodie and put her hood up. She walked with purpose. She found two police officers, and she asked them for help. They laughed at her and went the other direction. She doesn't hate the police, but there are those who make others look bad.

She found her hotel and prayed her husband was there. Part of her prayed that he never showed up. What she remembers a few hours later was that a strange man had entered her hotel room. She was so drunk that if he would have attacked her, she wouldn't be able to remember anything. He didn't attack her; he had found her husband on the side of the road, blacked-out drunk. He brought him to the hotel, thanks to the key card. He placed her husband on the bed and left. That was it. God was watching for sure.

They finished their trip and headed home.

Time to be an adult again.

My sweet girl didn't know that working with at-risk youth in a home setting without healing herself first was going to be so detrimental to her own health and well-being. While she did an amazing job with her teens (some of whom are still in contact with her after she left the field), pieces of her were breaking.

I can write a separate book on her memories from working in residential care, but right now, this is about her. Besides, she loved her kids and wouldn't want to shame them in any way. Just a little snippet of things she endured while she worked.

She dealt with her teens running away, drug use, overdosing, self-harm, sexual activity under the roof, abortions, riots, lots of yelling and destructing property—and those were just from the kids to each other.

She had a few kids who scarred her with biting, spitting on her, shoving her into doors and walls, crashing cars, shattering glass, tackling a kid before they were hit by a car, and having them threaten her job because she put hands on them.

She also had kids who grew up into amazing adults and kept in contact with her. It makes life seem worth it when you don't lose contact from those who are important.

But in between the tent years of working a lot, she herself was dying, and her marriage was falling apart.

It started with her working the overnight shift so she could be home with her kids during the day. Her daughter was in a private preschool, and her son was in second grade.

When my sweet girl would come home from work, she would drop her kids off where they needed to be and come home to rest, then she would do the mom thing.

Her husband worked for a good company and made decent money. He had the typical 9-5 job, and when he would come home, he would do something on his motorcycle or do guy things. He always had to be busy, and to be honest, if she sat around after working, she felt she was in trouble because she didn't want to do anything.

During the time working the overnights, she met someone who turned her life upside down. It wasn't on purpose, but there was an attraction that couldn't be denied and so started unsorted feelings.

The most amazing part of her feelings was that she saw this person as who they were. Her feelings were so conflicted because she was married, and one did not just have feeling for someone else; but at the same time, you couldn't fight the laws of attraction. She saw her in such a way that was protective, which she didn't feel from her husband in a long time. No, this isn't a typo, I said *her*.

There was no denying this attraction, and she did speak to her husband about it. I don't know why she did, but it happened.

So while working, being a wife and mother, my sweet angel was trying to find herself. I still don't know why she felt so lost. It may have something to do with never having closure with past traumas, and it continued to surface.

One thing about my girl is her need to feel loved. She wasn't into drugs, and when she did drink, it would only be socially, even though she did drink in excess at that. However, having someone love you for you and not hurt you is a scary thing.

Her husband agreed to let her find herself, but both went to the desert on one last trip as a "farewell" tour trip. She and her husband would go to the desert a lot; however this trip is important for the timeline. They had a great time, until they went for one last ride before heading home, and he rode with such speed on his bike, she couldn't keep up on her quad. She ended up losing him, and when she went to find her way back, she crashed her quad. She was not injured but had to find her way back to camp. They had already been riding for thirty minutes, so this was going to be a journey coming back. She began to walk—did I mention this was in June? She was in full riding gear and had her CamelBak full of water. Her thought was to find the road. She walked and kept thinking that she found people; she would run up to them, and they would be trees. It was that hot, she thought she was seeing people. Eventually, she saw tall telephone poles and began to walk toward them. She wasn't sure how long she had been walking at this point, but she was tired and hot. Full riding gear was not fun to walk in the desert heat with.

As she was walking, my sweet girl went on to think about her life thus far and couldn't believe she was here, going to die, in the desert due to the heat. She would never see her kids again.

When she felt like sitting and just waiting for someone to find her, she noticed a car with lights on top. It was the sheriff. The sheriff got out of his car and asked her name. She told him, and the sheriff told her that her husband had called to put out a search party for her. They gave her water and told her that if she wasn't found within a few minutes, they would have dispatched the chopper. A fucking chopper, that's a joke. He did this shit on purpose. Her husband wanted to be the hero, save his wife from dying in the desert. Didn't work.

They packed up their stuff and drove home; she had to work that night. She showed up, and her friend was just getting off shift. There were fireworks when they looked at each other, but the closest thing to anything was her friend walking up behind her to get close and whispered in her ear. Nothing happened, but my sweet girl wanted to be turned around to be kissed. She needed it, craved it. They remained professional.

Another night at work, and they both were there talking late into the night. All the clients were sleeping soundly; this was due to the high dose of medication each one was on. My sweet girl was sitting in the office chair, trying to do some homework before the bed check while talking to her forbidden crush. Her crush got up and walked toward her and stood behind her. She kissed her on top of the head and began to rub her shoulders, and while some may think that they went right at it on the desk, they didn't. They did explore a bit with their mouths on each other, and the feeling that was shooting through my heartbroken girl was the most amazing thing she had felt for a long time. It lasted a few minutes, and then her crush went home. They made plans to go out to get to know each other a bit.

They went on a few dates, nothing serious, to see what would come out of it; but of course, nothing happened. Her husband, while being "supportive," also was sabotaging her finding herself. He told her she was bipolar since mental illness ran in her family. My confused girl believed him.

The most absurd part of it was when she went to talk to a doctor about what has been going on, he immediately prescribed medication for bipolar. *Hey, man, fuck you!* Way to push scripts on someone after just one meeting.

My sweet girl started taking medication and felt worse when she was on them. Probably because she wasn't fucking crazy; she was damaged due to others stepping on her constantly.

Her friendship with her friend continued, but only in a professional manner again; it was a choice made by her friend. She told my sweet girl that she was no good for my sweet girl and would end up hurting her as well and told her to figure out what she wanted in life for her and no one else.

This is where I would say her first break happened. She didn't go to the hospital, she would never self-harm, but her thoughts and feeling were bubbling, and she just wanted to scream at those who deserved it. Growing up in the family she did, that wasn't allowed.

Go to church, be respectful, let your family walk on you, shut the fuck up, be a wife, a mother, a psychotic bitch, work hard, eat and drink your feelings.

Now, I was noticing a dark change in my sweet girl, and she also was noticing a change in her son. Her son was defiant all the time. Again, it was brushed off as "boys will be boys," and at times, her family took it as he had a hard life because his mom was a teenage mom. The fuck? We are now way past that, but she stayed quiet.

My sweet girl needed a break and happen to have reconnected with a childhood friend and went to see her in a different state. They spent a few days together and went to see a concert together. When she got home, she got her first tattoo. It was huge and on her lower back. It was for her "girlfriend" from work. During that vacation, my girl knew she and her friend wouldn't be together, but she gave her the strength to attempt to heal.

This was the second person who attempted to help my girl heal. The first, remember, was her husband.

So again, life seemed to calm down, and routine took place. Work, school, and kids. Desert trips with quads and spending time with her best friend who lived across the street.

This is a good time to bring this family into your life. They were a married couple. They had one son who was a year younger than my sweet girl's daughter.

The husband worked, and she stayed at home. They were good Christians who treated everyone with love and respect. They accepted my sweet girl as she was.

My sweet girl and her friend would go on walks with the kids and drink coffee; they would shop and sit in the front yard with the kids and the kiddie pool while they tanned and read magazines. The greatest thing about this was it was a normal existence. But when my sweet girl would go back home, she never knew what kind of day she was going to have with her husband.

For now, she kept that quiet; she didn't want to scare off someone whom she felt close to.

This friendship was beautiful and pure. It is still beautiful to this day over a decade later, but we will get to that.

During the time of their budding friendship, my sweet girl was still attempting to figure out who she was—and I know I keep repeating that, but little do you know, many years later, she would still attempt to figure out the whys in her life.

My sweet girl worked for a few years and then decided to go back to school. She found a program to earn her bachelors of science—get it, BS. It is total bullshit. She would go to school at night and then go straight to work. It was draining on her. She put her head down and worked. I believe this is where the cracks really started to show.

During that time of working, one of her facilities was being shut down, and she was being transferred to an entirely new company. Guess who was there? Her tattoo, forbidden crush friend. They remained professional, but something about the two of them in the same house working again was messing with her head, even if it was just in passing that they saw each other.

What no one that worked with my sweet girl knew was that her home life was going back to being abusive and angry. It was always

49

back and forth. Her husband was abusive. I believe that her husband wanted to be a good husband, but sometimes he just lost his shit and didn't know how to communicate without hurting. My sweet girl wanted her husband to love her and not hurt her. She was already dealing with damage from others, why her husband?

Sitting at work, she received a song from her husband in her e-mail. She already knew this song and this band, but when he sent this to her, it shook her up so emotionally, and this was the turning point. The song was "Hate Me" by Blue October. She loved this band, so she was pissed that he decided to use this song to attempt to make things better. *No asshole, what you did was give her permission to say fuck you!*

If you ask her now how she felt, she will tell you that a long time ago, she wanted people to hate her for not being able to shut up about the abuse and just smile. She wanted to hate people for abusing her and treating her like trash, but in the end, she hated herself for how they made her feel. All the fucking time!

Her soul was broken, but she didn't want to give up on her marriage because that was not what you do. She wanted to go to therapy with her husband, but he was against it. He even laughed at the idea.

During her night classes, she thrived on doing well; she even wrote papers for some of her classmates, and she maintained a 3.5 GPA at the time. This was between working and doing the mom/wife losing her mind thing.

The best part of her program she was a part of was the group of friends she made. Years later, they talk on social media; but this group helped her when she was at her lowest and kept my sweet girl going with the prospect of a bright future.

Things were normal—well, routine. Routine was not even close to being normal, but to her, she kept smiling and working toward her soon-to-be perfect life. Then, one day, one class, they walked in her life and changed it forever. Two guys who were as beautiful on the inside as they were out.

She sat in class and couldn't stop staring and smiling at the two of them. She held on to every word during presentations. Instead of the messy "I don't care" attitude, she started taking her time getting ready for school. She would leave early to try and meet up with them. They all became friends, and it was innocent enough. There was flirting, but nothing to write home about. Back at home, things were changing as well.

Her husband decided to go into the Border Patrol and would be gone for a few months for training. This meant she was doing the mom, work, and student thing by herself, and with the help of her mom, who would come by and watch the kids while they slept.

Again, routine. The times she would talk to her husband on the phone, it was the usual; and sometimes, when she would miss him so much, it started a fight because she needed to handle life and stop being a pussy. Now, their son began to become so defiant toward her. He even snuck out the front door and ran away. She got in the car when she noticed; he made it down the street in just his socks. I don't think any kid ran so fast back home. He was driving her crazy, but again, there were excuses on why he was acting this way.

The more her life at home seemed to be falling apart, the more she continued to inch closer to her classmates. Now, the only one who didn't drive her nuts was her daughter. The most beautiful baby, she knew they would be best friends. She wanted to be sure she protected and loved her daughter in a way she wasn't protected.

After class one day, my sweet girl went home and noticed there was no power connecting to her computer. She could have called anyone, but she called her classmate. She asked for advice on how to fix it. While they were on the phone, she turned into an electrician. If you meet my sweet girl, you will know she is nothing close to an electrician or should be allowed to work on anything that can take her life. No one was there to help her, and she needed to do what was needed to fix shit.

She knocked herself on her ass with a jolt, stupid sweet girl. Her friend on the other line was trying not to laugh, but he did, and then she did. She needed that.

Her husband was going to be gone for her birthday, so she had some friends come over to celebrate. It was fun, and a quiet event. Her two classmates that she wanted to come didn't show, but she was determined to celebrate with them.

One night after class, she happened to run into one of her classmates at the gas station. What started here wasn't intentional, but at this moment in time, she was broken, severely. She didn't do drugs but did like to drink. She asked if they could go get a beer, and he invited her back to his place.

They sat in his room and had a few beers. Then he pulled out his pipe, and this was the first time she had ever smoked pot. It relaxed her. She felt so calm, but not in a way where she didn't know what was going on. They left to go get some food, and on the ride there, Macy Gray came on the radio. There was a connection that was felt, and when they got back to his place—well, she had one of the most spiritual experiences to date, but she also betrayed herself. She became a cheater. This wasn't meant to happen and no details. She is ashamed of what she did and, to be honest, thought it would only be once. A "what happens in Vegas" sort of deal. It didn't happen only once. It continued to happen while her husband was at the academy.

She had changed. She was still playing the good wife, mommy, student by day, and after class sometimes, the two of them would hang out and release tension. She knew it was wrong, but she couldn't stop.

Now, let me stop you right here with your thoughts of her being a slut and how dare she do that. Was it wrong? Yes, absolutely, and she knew it. To this day, she is ashamed of it; but at the time, she was broken. If you have never been broken by the hands or words of someone else, good for you. And second, shut the fuck up. Not everyone judges, but this was the one point in her life where she felt as bad as she possibly could.

The time had come to go to her husband's graduation. It was a family affair. Her mom, stepdad, son, daughter, and, of course, herself would pile into a van and drive to New Mexico. Longest road trip ever. They did make it, and while it was a nice graduation, she didn't really care to see her husband. She knew that things wouldn't change when they got home. She was texting her friend while on the trip. Nothing incriminating, but nonetheless, she wanted and needed the contact. No one knew about it. After the graduation ceremony, she and her husband fucked in the rental van, in a Walmart parking lot. Classy. It was the only time they could get any space. She felt no connection.

I don't remember what started it, but there was a fight on the way home. An argument between her mom and her husband. They were always at odds. Her mom and stepdad always felt her husband's parenting was subpar because he was hard on the kids. He wasn't abusive to the kids, but he didn't put up with shit.

My sweet girl couldn't wait to get home, and go to class.

Things from this point on only got worse. Once he got home, she became more distant and sometimes wouldn't come home. She would be with him, her friend from class. They were even a part of the same internship program. The secrets continued to build, but she couldn't and refused to tell him she was done. Deep down, she was afraid of being judged.

Then one day, while she was napping, her husband brought an e-mail that was written by her to her classmate. He had printed it out he put a key logger on her computer to get her password. It didn't go into detail, but you would have to be an idiot to not know the content. Besides being shocked, she went into self-preservation mode. Instead of coming clean to him, she lied and continued to lie. She didn't know what to do.

Trust was broken, and yes, she was sad, but at the time, she didn't really care.

When she first realized that there was no turning back was during a weekend she was supposed to take the kids to a birthday party. This was for her best friend's son. It was at his grandparents' house, so they were going to have to drive. She ran to the store to get a present, and then she picked up a lighter. A single lighter. This was for the girls at the recovery home she interned at. She realized she needed one during their smoke breaks, and it was just a way to help them. No big deal. When she got home, he looked at the receipt and began to yell about all the extra things she bought. It was just a lighter. He took her car keys and her wallet and told her she couldn't go to the party. He took the phones, so she couldn't call her best friend. Big mistake. There was a knock on the door. Her best friend left the party, drove over to the house, and pushed her way through. Her best friend asked my sad girl if she was okay. The only answer she could give was a sad yes. Her best friend left at my sweet girl's response that she was okay. She knew he had to get back to her own family.

During the holidays was when things really came to a head. During Thanksgiving, since she had to work, she stayed home while he took the kids to his family's house up north. What you don't know was they shared a cell phone, and he took it. So she made sure she let her friends know he had it, and she went to get her own. He felt this was a crossed line and that she shouldn't have her own phone. They were in their mid-twenties, and he was refusing to allow her to get her own phone. What a joke. Of course, it didn't go over well.

Christmas happened, and there was awkward fighting at her parents' house; he yelled at her in front of the family, and for that, she sunk back in her shell. But what did her family do? Absolutely nothing. They ignored it. Everyone, except for her aunt. She did ask if my sweet girl was okay. All she could do was say "I guess so." She didn't want to ask for anyone's help. Remember when she was molested? What happened then? Nothing. When they got home, the fighting continued, and he kept kicking her on the ground as she cried, begging him to love her. She just wanted to be loved so badly, without any restrictions.

During New Year's Eve, she didn't spend it with her husband or her kids. To her, this was her stand. She wasn't going to take it anymore. She met up with a friend whom her husband didn't know and spent the night at his place. She told her husband she was having a girl's night, but she wasn't with any girls, just one guy. He fucked her good; she didn't even know this could happen, and again, she felt guilty after. She went home and acted as though she had a great time with her girlfriends.

Back to routine, but this time it was different. She had to watch her every move, even at work and school. While at school, the guy whom she spent the night with on NYE told her that her husband had messaged him, saying she was unstable and to stay away from her. She couldn't figure out how he found out, but that was the last time she ever saw him. Eh, whatever.

Her husband then began to show up at her school. He showed up one night and parked behind her car. One of her classmates was walking her out to her car. This classmate and she were friends only. He was the other part of the good-looking pair. She loved him dearly—and to this day, still does—she knows this one night he saved her life.

While going to the car, she noticed her husband, and he began to ask questions on who her friend was and what he was doing with her. What her friend didn't know was her husband could turn violent quick.

She knew something was up. She asked where his gun was, and he said it was under the seat. Her friend told her husband that this was her school and that this wasn't the way to handle this situation. He spoke to her husband and convinced him to drive home, and he convinced her to go home as well to talk about things.

They both drove home, where her mom was watching the kids. As soon as they got in the house, they began to fight in the kitchen, and her mom tried to smooth things over. He called his wife, my girl, a whore and a slut, so she grabbed a steak knife and told him she would just slice her wrists right then to end it all. At that moment in time, she was in so much pain, she just wanted to die; but she loved her kids so much, she would never leave them. She went into her room and sobbed. She was exhausted, emotionally and mentally.

Back to routine, back to school, work, life. While doing all these routine things, she was trying to get the courage to leave, but she couldn't. She didn't want to fail, and divorce was failing.

She decided to go to therapy for herself, because he refused to go with her. She spoke about her childhood and opened to the therapist. She felt that she could get the help she wanted and needed. One day after therapy, she came home, and her husband asked what she talked about.

She told him it was none of his business. He lost his shit. He began to yell at her, in their bedroom, and right outside were her kids and her best friend's son. They were all playing together when her husband grabbed his gun and began to yell at her that it was time to end it all. My sweet scared girl jumped on their bed and got in the fetal position. She knew that if he shot her, there was no position that would protect her. But he didn't shoot. When she looked up after it had gotten quiet, she noticed the gun was resting next to her. She wasn't sure if he wanted her to shoot him or herself. To this day, she wonders what life would have been like if she did either one of those.

At her next therapy appointment, she told her therapist what had happened, and she told her she would send a squad car by for a welfare check when she got home. As soon as she got home, her husband yelled at her for disclosing that information about the gun because he had a job with clearance and could lose it. His job, that was what he was concerned about. Fuck off!

The next day, he apologized and said he would try and work on his temper and try to work on their relationship, if she was willing. She was willing. Just like that. But this wasn't the end of the abuse. Things went back to "normal," and she told him, finally, that she wanted a divorce; but he wouldn't budge, so she decided to ignore him in every way possible. She shut down.

One day, when she was at her internship, he called and demanded to speak to her. He said he went and closed the bank account and that she had to ask him for money because it was a joint account. She was earning her own money due to working in a new residential center for teens, so she didn't understand this tactic; but it worked, and she was scared.

She told him she had to go back to work with her clients at the recovery house she was doing her hours with. He said if she hung up, he would drive over there and handle it. Her protective side came out, and she walked out. She didn't want to put these ladies in danger.

Her friend from school, the one whom she had the affair with, was in the same program for his hours; and he followed her in his car as she drove home. He kept asking her if she needed a ride home, but she didn't want to put his life in danger. So she walked. It took about an hour to walk home. As she was walking up her driveway and up the steps to her house, her husband opened the door; but she began to take her clothes off outside. She completely stripped down and walked to her bedroom without saying a word.

She lay on the bed naked and said, "Do what you want. I'm done." Her husband felt the best thing to do was to shove pills down her throat because she was having an "episode." How about her life was a complete fucking joke and no one would help her? But you could blame her as well. She never screamed loud enough or long enough.

That weekend was a normal weekend. She went to get her nails done, and they were going to come home to watch some football. On the way home, she was driving and said she was going to take the kids to her parents' house for the weekend for a break. She needed a rest. He took that as if she was going to take the kids away from him. He grabbed the steering wheel out of her hand and crashed the car into the curb. This wasn't the first car accident when he decided to be angry with her. This was just the first one with the kids in it. She didn't go to her parents' house.

She tried to get her brother to come over and help since he was the closest. His girlfriend at the time, now her sister-in-law, told her he couldn't come over because she didn't want him to go to jail for helping his sister. Wow, what a family. Of course, my sweet broken girl was put last again.

Things of course didn't get better from there. Their son was in football, and during a banquet for the end of the year, they fought—huge—and it was embarrassing. They both drove separately because they couldn't even be in the same car without fighting. When they both raced home, she had the kids; she decided that was it, and she was going to her parents' house. When they got to the house, she locked the kids in her truck to go inside; but her husband had locked her out. She keyed in, and he began to shove the door on her, and she used her strength to open the door. When she got in to get some items, he went through the other door and could open the truck. He took her purse out of the truck and began to go through it. He started to take all her money and cut up her credit and debit cards. She jumped on his back while he was doing this. She began to beat on him to let go of her purse. He shook her off, and she fell to the ground. He began to kick her while she was on the ground. She could get her stuff, and they both calmed down enough for them to conclude that a break was needed. He ended up leaving for the night, and she was at the house with the kids. She looked in the mirror after he left. She had a handprint around her neck. She took a picture of it but didn't know what she would do with it. She had bruises up and down her arms. How did her life get to this point? In her mind, she would be in trouble for touching him as well, so there was no going to the cops.

The next night, her husband came barging in the door and said that he paid for the house and that he wouldn't leave. He said he would sleep on the couch. For some reason, my lost girl said she would sleep on the couch, partly so she could be next to the kids.

The sleeping on the couch only continued for a little while. Eventually, it was decided that she would go up and live with her parents, and she would get the kids on the weekends—which was decided because she as a mom wanted the kids to be stable in their own beds. She wanted to be sure the kids were always stable while they worked out their own shit.

No matter the choices in her life, her kids came first. She always wanted to be sure they were happy, and at the time, she couldn't afford the bills at the house; otherwise, she would have stayed.

Since she was at her parents' house, it was over an hour's drive to get to work. There were times when she would have to pull sixteen-hour shifts and would just sleep at work. She buried herself in her work and then spend time with her kids on the weekend. She was a mess, and unfortunately, she didn't trust anyone.

Over time, it was easier to not go home, but something had to be done. The two of them had a serious talk and figured out divorce was going to be the best way to get it done.

The plan was to go to the courthouse together and file for divorce. They had enough time and space to calm down and really think about life and what was best for everyone. A few days before they were going to go to court, my sweet girl was headed back up to her parents' house. As she was driving, she had a bad feeling in the pit of her stomach when she passed the hospital in town, but she couldn't pinpoint why.

There was crappy service headed up the hill, so she didn't know her cell phone had rang, and she didn't get the message until she made it to her parents' house. She checked her voice mail, and there was a static message talking to her, a man's voice she didn't know. All it said was her husband had been in a motorcycle accident, and he was on a life flight to the hospital. What a fucking asshole, stupid, motherfucker, manipulating prick! She knew this was a ploy to make her stay, but of course, she worried; he was her children's father and wouldn't wish any harm to him, not that he would take that sort of consideration for her.

When she arrived at the hospital, she was told that he was alive but injured badly. If he hadn't had his full body leather suit on, he would have died. Apparently, he did some sort of superman dive over a car. There was so much to process, and she was still dealing with her feelings of getting a divorce.

She took his phone and called people she thought he would want to know. His mom and his sister drove down to be there for him.

While his mom and his sister were there, my angry, frustrated girl made sure the kids were taken care of, like she always does. The one thing she didn't do was clean the house; which, of course, was a disaster. I remember his mom getting angry with her because she refused to clean the house. She didn't live there anymore.

My girl became stressed out still trying to go to school and to raise her kids. One night, she skipped class and ended up spending the night with the guy whom she had an affair with. He was house-sitting. They fucked in the hot tub. She slept on the couch and left in the morning. There was no feeling toward it, just something that was. She needed it.

Her husband was in the hospital for a while, and after, they did go to court together to file papers. Everything was good; they wanted it easy. She ended up giving him the house because she didn't make enough to pay the mortgage. What she didn't realize was as easy as things were, this would start an uphill battle to last for years.

She was a dumb, stupid girl and didn't ask for alimony or child support. Nothing. She even had the kids at the house, again to remain stable. Little did she know her sacrifice for their safety and health would end up hurting her later.

After they filed, which was calm and civil, both decided they wanted to stay friends, which at the time seemed like it could work.

My sweet girl lived at her parents' house and looked for a place to live. She had this sense of freedom she never felt before. She wasn't sure what to do. She went on Craigslist to find a roommate.

She found a roommate with odd requirements, but this place was close to her work, and it seemed to work for a while. There were occasions when her ex-husband and she would go to see concerts together. During the time after they filed for divorce, they went to a few shows, and there were times when they went to the beach together, as a family with the kids. It seemed to work.

The relationship with her roommate was weird, and he kept making rules for her, like they were together. She didn't like it, so she stayed away a lot of the time. The times she didn't have her kids, she would work or go out and party. There were times when she would sit at home and drink her vodka drinks and attempt to eat her weight in Taco Bell.

My girl decided to try and meet people. She went on a dating website. She was paired with a guy from high school, and from what she remembered, he was always nice to her, and cute. He had just started seeing someone, so she moved on. To her that was funny, as adults' things changed from when you are growing up, so who knew what would have happened if he did say "Let's meet up." But God had a plan, and while there were so many tests, he brought her to her husband.

During her work days, my hardworking girl always tried her best. She wanted to be sure that she didn't date or make friends at work. Her heart was hard, and she figured if she could just focus on her job and her kids, life would get easier. Life doesn't always go as planned. She had been a part of this company for a few weeks now, but going back to her first days training, she was walking down the hall, and there he was. A very fit, beautiful man with dark skin and long brown hair. My girl knew that was it, her life was over; she had to get to know him. So over time, she made sure they worked the same days, or when she would look at the schedule, she would put herself on call so that way they could work together. She never told anyone about this—and to be honest, the first time they ever spoke, he teased her. She was trying too hard to make an impression, and he called her out.

She didn't get offended; in fact, she thought it was refreshing. Someone who could still be truthful to her and not be a dick. Don't get me wrong, he was an asshole, but not a dick. Yes, there is a difference. When you work in close quarters with people, it's hard to not make friends, and she made a few. The ones she made friends with were not part of the popular crowd, or the clique. She liked them. One of the girls she made friends with was close with the guy whom she secretly liked. They were only friends, and so my brilliant girl could convince her friend to invite him to a birthday shindig she was having. They all were going to the local bar to shoot pool and drink, a lot.

My sassy girl met everyone at her new crush's house, and they drove to the bar together. There weren't that many people, but she didn't drive her own car; she ended up going with her friend, her supervisor from work, and his friend. Her crush and another guy drove separately. They had a lot of fun and played pool all night, and the beers kept flowing. There was even a bet during the pool game, which was lost by my sassy girl. She had to do push-ups in the bar, in her dress. Challenge accepted. The night ended, and they all went their separate ways. She got back in the car with her friend, supervisor, and his friend. She was in the back seat with the friend.

The plan was to go to the casino to play poker. She figured, why not? On the way there, the friend put his sausage fingers on her leg and began to rub his hand up her thigh. She shook him off, and he continued. She told her supervisor that she wanted to be taken back to her car. The slimy weasel sitting next to her ran his fucking hand up her leg and said, "Just stay" Get the fuck out of here, *just stay?*

Her supervisor took her back to her car, but she was still not sober enough to drive. She knocked on her crush's door, and he was there with another coworker. The two of them were just bullshitting and invited her in. She sat on the couch, and her crush offered to make her food to soak up the night. She accepted. She had fallen asleep on the couch. He woke her up and placed a bowl of rice and veggies on her lap. She ate it half-asleep. The coworker left, and her crush asked her if she would like to use his bed to sleep in.

Her subconscious was angry because in her mind, she thought that even after all that, he was just trying to get in her panties. She told him the couch was fine and fell into a deep sleep. Her alarm went off at 5:00 a.m., but she ended up throwing her phone across the room. When she finally woke up, it was 5:45 a.m., and she jolted out of bed. She had to be at work at six. She had no clothes with her and needed to shower. She was gathering her stuff to leave, and she noticed a pair of pajamas on the table next to where she was sleeping. She was also covered with a blanket, and in his room was her crush, sleeping soundly. She didn't remember the night, but she did know that he didn't try anything. There was just a feeling that one got when they knew if they had sex. There was no sex that night. She drove home, which was fifteen minutes away, and did a sailor shower and drove to work. She got to work right at 6:30. She had to work a double that day, and she was hungover. This day would be fun.

She spent the day texting her crush, thanking him for the night, and was trying to see if he wanted to hang out again. He kept trying to talk up their coworker who was at his house that night as well. My clueless girl didn't get the hint; she really liked this guy. It was more than looks. She liked him because he didn't take advantage of her, and that was huge. She hadn't felt safe in long time, and that simple act was huge.

Even though she was tired, she knew she wanted to see him that night, and he finally agreed to hang out. He told her he would cook, and she could bring whatever she wanted to drink. So she brought vodka. He didn't drink, but he made her a drink.

They sat and talked for hours. His food was delicious. She found out he played football with Tom Brady, and that he was from the Bay Area. She hated Tom Brady, being a Chargers fan, but she did absolutely adore the Bay Area and told him she always wanted to live there.

She had to work the next day, and his roommate was gone, so he offered for her to sleep on the couch. It turned in to a bed. They watched a movie until it was time to go to sleep. One of her favorites, *Pretty Woman*.

It was time to go to sleep. He put his arms around her, and she liked that. He began to whisper something in her ear. She turned over to figure out what he was saying. That was it, her life was over—or just beginning. I won't get into details of their night together, only because this is her husband now. And we will get to that, but those details of that night don't need to be said.

So at that moment, they were friends, with benefits. She liked him a lot, and he was hard to read. She didn't know what was going to happen with him. They kept their friendship quiet; he didn't tell anyone his business. The great thing was the clique at work hated him. They thought he was a horrible counselor and spoke so much shit. She liked that they didn't like him. More to herself.

Their friendship continued in silence. She had other friends but nothing like him. One weekend, he was going to Colorado to be the best man at a wedding. So she was free for the weekend. She invited her coworker to hang out. She really liked her new man, and so hanging out with her co-worker was just that. They watched a movie at her place and ate crap pizza. She kept the door of her room open so that way, he wouldn't get the wrong idea. Her man called from Colorado while her friend was over.

Her friend became agitated that she would talk about her man, and what he didn't know was that they were sleeping together. He just thought my smart girl was crushing on her friend while this douche was attempting to get in her pants. Never happened.

The greatest story came when her new man came back from Colorado. They were lying in bed together, and the douche called her. She put him on speaker. He invited her over to hang out, and she kept telling him she was busy. He was drunk, and when he was going to hang up, she overheard him talking shit about her. He kept talking to his friend about her being a whore and a tease. Then, as his friend started calling her names, this douche had the nerve to come to her defense. My angry girl had heard enough.

The next time she had to work with this guy, she confronted him. She told him she heard everything that he had said.

His response? "I was talking shit about you so that way I can defend your honor." The fuck? What kind of sick logic was that?

After that, they worked together, but nothing more.

My healing girl wanted to introduce her kids to her "man." As friends, of course. So one weekend, they hung out at her apartment. Her roommate was gone, so she figured it would be a nice weekend. The kids slept with her in her room, and he slept on the couch. The next morning, the four of them were hanging out and getting ready to take the kids back to their dad. He was sitting on the couch without his shirt on, and she was sitting on the floor.

In walked her roommate. He never met her "man" before, so she introduced them. They went on their day, and all seemed great. That was until her roommate messaged her after she went to drop off the kids at their dad. The message said he needed to talk to her. She had a bad feeling, but what would her roommate do, he wasn't her man.

She got to the apartment, alone; she dropped off her "man" so he could get stuff ready for the week. When she walked in the door, her roommate began to yell at her. He called her a slut and a whore for bringing a man around her children and fucking him while they were under the same roof. She became upset and defensive and tried explaining herself to this prick. He was just her roommate and had no right to judge her. She told him that she was moving out. He could afford the place on his own, so it wasn't a big deal.

The next weekend, her dad and her man came to help her pack her belongings and drive them back to her parents' house. She was real sick of going home, but that's where she was at. While she was "living" there, she spent more time with her man since his place was closer to work.

The more they were together, the more she never wanted to leave. He made her feel so safe and loved. Her ex-husband knew they were friends and seemed okay with it. He had to travel to Germany for a trip, so he allowed her man to watch the kids at his house for the week. There was no pay offered; he did it because he cared. She had to work a lot, and they didn't have day care, so this was the best option, and the cheapest.

During that week, nothing naughty happened; it would have been disrespectful. Once her ex came back from Germany, life went back to normal. She would bounce between her parents' house and her man's house. She would work and spend time with her kids. Things were working out. She was starting to feel happy.

I don't know what exactly happened that made her snap, but it did, and one day she felt that this wasn't going to work. She was scared that they were getting too close, which part of her wanted. Her dumbass went to her so-called friend/supervisor and asked for advice. She listened to what he had to say, talking so much shit about a man whom she was falling hard for, and didn't want to let her true feelings known.

The greatest thing about this, her friend/supervisor had been fucking two of her coworkers at the same time, and they didn't know. She didn't either, but she listened to what he had to say because he was "the smartest guy in the room."

One night after work, she went and wrote a brilliant e-mail, accusing her man of all sorts of shit that was not true, but she ended it with how much she cared about him. The response from him was mean and vile. She deserved it.

She ended up staying with her ex at his house and having nightmares about this man whom she just threw away.

What a stupid girl. She ended up being miserable, and for the next few weeks she sulked and walked around work so angry. What was wrong with her? She tried calling him to apologize, and it kept going to voice mail.

She didn't know he was at the gym, and he was breaking the heavy bags. Literally breaking them. He hulked out on the poor bags.

Almost a month went by, and one night, my sad girl went to a bar/club with her girlfriend. She needed to drink and dance. They danced into the night, and the next morning she received a text from her "man"

It said that if she wanted to talk to him, he would be at the gym. She got all her shit together and drove as fast as she could. She had received the message a few hours after it was sent. She thought she would miss him. He was there. He had this face, which scared her, but he told her to sit and wait while he finished his set.

She told him she was so sorry, and if he could forgive her. He didn't say much, but he asked her to lunch. Huh? That was it, nothing more. He told her that she said what she needed to say, and he didn't want her to grovel. She had to work in an hour, but they did have lunch, and he dropped her off at work in her car. He didn't have a car, and he chose to walk or bike everywhere. Kept him in shape.

After work, he picked her up, and they went to his place. Now, he had a temporary roommate who wanted to fuck him. He never did though. She wasn't happy to see my happy girl enter the apartment.

That night they didn't fuck but made love. Making love, what is that? It's a connection, and they had it.

The holidays were rolling around, and she was to spend Thanksgiving with him. What about her kids? Well, now, she didn't realize since there wasn't a court order and she thought she and her ex-husband were civil. What was happening was because of her work schedule—she needed to survive since she didn't ask for money from him—he was slowly taking time away. She was seeing her kids on Mondays and every other weekend. She didn't know this wasn't normal.

For some reason, in her head, she thought she was doing right by her kids allowing her ex keep them at the house; they were in a safe, stable environment. She wanted the best for her babies always.

So, before you judge her for being a shitty mom, walk in her shoes, just for a second; besides, no one can make her feel more inadequate at being a mom than her.

Thanksgiving was interesting. My sweet girl met a friend of her man's, and she knew right away there was something bubbling underneath this friend. She noticed the friend was a little jealous, but at the same time, she couldn't say anything. This was a friend from years ago, and maybe that was just how her face sat.

After everyone left for the night, both went to bed, and he told her he loved her. Don't know what brought that on, but she vowed to never let him go again, and she has stuck by that till this day.

At that time, people still didn't know they were a couple; it would be about a year before it came out. She tried to bring him around to family events, and she was getting mixed reviews. Well, no—her family judged him, badly. She couldn't figure it out. He was a nice guy who loved her and treated her with respect, but he was judged, and do you think this would stop? Nope, he would be judged almost tent years after they were together.

Her job at the residential facility was going well, and he moved on to be a bartender at a new restaurant that was opening. He first started to tend bar back in the Bay Area, and he needed a change. He loved his job and made decent money doing it. Life was looking up. My working girl still lived at her parents' house but spent majority of her time with him when they weren't working and when she wasn't with her kids. She had become the fun weekend mom. She didn't want to be the weekend mom, but she was still so scarred and afraid of her ex-husband that she didn't push to get the kids more. She didn't want him to retaliate.

The holidays passed, and Valentines weekend was coming up. They didn't have any plans because still no one knew they were together, and it was a big weekend at the restaurant. So they both were going to work. One day, while my clumsy girl was preparing lunch for her teens, she gave herself her own concussion. Still laugh at this, but it was serious. She hit her head on a kitchen cabinet so hard that it closed, opened, and closed again. It hurt. Her supervisor didn't send her to the ER and told her to put ice on it and finish her shift. She was dizzy and was falling over, but she finished her shift.

When her love had picked her up from work, they went out to eat, and she was falling asleep at the table. He took her to the ER, and yes, it was a concussion. She was told to stay home from work for a few days, but not to sleep, or to have someone take care of her. Her love had to work that weekend, so he got her all the supplies she needed, and he would check in on her. He bought her a book, and she tried to read it, couldn't.

When she did get back to work, she was chastised and told she was faking her injury to have the weekend off. Seriously? She was in bed all weekend, but there was no romance to do with it. Her supervisor needed to lay off the crack. But seriously, he was an addict, and yet he was the one that was liked and trusted to be in charge.

Before you get mad that I said that, listen, we have all our own issues, but for someone to act perfect while you are dealing with your own demons, it's crap. She lost all respect for this guy. He was plain ignorant.

My tired girl was sick of traveling back and forth between her parents' house and her love's house. She couldn't move in because it wasn't his house to make the decision. She did have a friend who was living at home, but they had a studio apartment she could rent out. She decided to take her friend up on that offer. Usually offers from friends are too good to be true. This was the same. While living in the house, her mom had asked if there was any room for her to move in there as well.

Since this isn't about her family, there is no need to bring them up, but this time it's important. Her mom and stepdad were taking a break. Since her grandfather died, her stepdad's father, he had become lost and angry. He would take it out on her mom. So she decided to run away and live with her daughter.

Guess who else moved in? Her love. This was unplanned, but remember the temporary roommate? She ruined his living arrangement, and he had nowhere to go. So my caring girl offered him to move in with her. She loved living with her love, and her kids would come over and spend the night. It was working, for a while.

Time went by, and things became awkward. My love didn't want to associate with her friend anymore due to different styles of living, and there was just drama. Her mom still lived there too, so she and her love and my girl looked for an apartment together.

They moved into a nice two-bedroom apartment with the intention that her mom would pay one-third of rent because she was staying there. She did for a while, and then her mom decided to go back home. My girl and her love tried to make it on their own, and for a while, they were doing okay.

Have you ever been going through life and then a train hits you? Well, get ready for a ride, and this train was in the form of her ex-husband.

It was over Christmas break, and he took their kids to the snow. Next thing I know, my concerned girl is getting a phone call from her stepdad and her mom telling her that her son had been abused by her ex-husband that and they needed to go to a lawyer to get custody of her son. Her ex had never been abusive toward the kids at that point. He was rough, and he made some mistakes regarding their son, but my girl would never say it was abuse. Apparently, during a trip to the snow, there was an ice ball thrown at their son's head, and it left a goose egg. So, this was the information from their son, and her parents ran with it. I can't remember exactly how they found out before her, but it happened.

Hindsight being 20/20, if she hadn't pursued this, life would be different, but she did.

After work one day, she met her parents at a family attorney's office. What she recalls was going over her experience with her ex-husband but also the lack of seeing her kids. The first step was the restraining order. Her ex-husband had no clue what was about to happen, and to be honest, she didn't want to hurt him, she never did, but her son was saying that he was being hurt, so this was the plan. Both kids were removed from his custody at the time, until court. When these court proceedings started, no one came to support my girl but her love. Her parents who started this didn't show up. Her brother, nope. She didn't blame her dad for not coming, only because he didn't want anything to do with this, and he didn't start this. He had always been neutral.

The attacks started, and the gloves came off. She tried using his abuse toward her to get an edge up, and he tried using her "mental" health to get an edge. The judge told both to knock this shit off. This went on for a long time. During the court proceedings, life at work became difficult, and she had to take time off to go to the court proceedings. She was stressed out, and one day during a staff meeting, she felt her face start to twitch. Her Bell's palsy came back, and that was just another thing to live with. It got to the point with her Bell's palsy that she needed to take a leave, and in dealing with all the drama, it became too much. Her love was there to protect her and keep her from losing her mind. During the time of her leave, her work was cutting hours, and she ended up being laid off.

During this time, my damaged girl became depressed and ate a lot. Her love would work and attempt to provide for the both. She was waiting for some disability to go through, and it seemed it took forever. She became insecure due to her paralyzed face. How could she do anything? This wasn't the first time, but hopefully the last.

In dealing with her own pain and sadness for allowing her stress to get this far, there was another issue.

In court, it was decided that her ex-husband could have visitation with their son. One day, he showed up at the apartment early. He didn't know that she was at home, and he attempted to bully his way in to the apartment to take their son. Her love and her ex-husband became physical, until my angry girl got involved. She threatened to call the cops. He called his lawyer.

This back and forth and not giving in to anything lasted a long time. They wouldn't stop fighting, but for now, she had her son living with her.

Their son was going to a school that was near where she was living, and it seemed the same issues that followed him since he was a little boy continued. He wouldn't focus and was getting in trouble. One day, he was walking home from school and ended up calling his mom from the Burger King. He was in the bathroom and had shit himself. He was stuck in the stall and was too embarrassed to leave. She and her love drove the two minutes, and her love went into the bathroom and wrapped a jacket around her son and escorted him out. People stared, but they didn't dare say anything. If you saw her love, you wouldn't say anything. He would kill you.

If she didn't already love him, this right there said it all. He loved her kids without strings. He didn't need to, he chose to.

My girl's Bell's palsy was better, and she could get a job doing data entry. For her, this was a nice change. She got the job through a temp agency. Since this was a temp job, she wasn't sure how long it would last, but she put her head down and worked. They liked her there, except the boss was a hard ass and didn't like drama. During the time she worked doing data entry, she would get phone calls all the time from her attorney about the custody case.

This only flew for so long, and she eventually was let go from her job. She was devastated, and she felt that she was a failure.

Now, her old job was hiring again, and they called her; she was hesitant because she knew upper management didn't give a shit about their employees. But it was a job, and she loved her kids she worked with. She would stay with this company for six years, and in those years, she would have to see more trauma than any normal person.

Since she was back at work, she tried to keep quiet about her personal life. She wanted to just work, and that was what she did. The custody issue was attempting to sort itself out, and her ex-husband had supervised visits. Her best friend conducted these visits. While you are thinking, it was messed up to have my girl's friend do the visits, she knew both, and she would be fair.

The visits went okay, and he could see their son more.

It was coming to be summer time, and there was a plan for her kids to go up north to see her ex-husband's family for a few weeks. They each got time to have vacation and just needed to give written notice.

While my girl was nervous, she had to allow this, but she didn't want it. She didn't trust him and knew something would happen. One of his neighbors called her one night and said that he was packing up his trailer and was doing this for hours. My girl knew he liked to be prepared when he went on trips, and legally, she couldn't do anything about it. She thanked the neighbor for the information.

While the kids were on vacation with their dad, my girl and her love tried to have some normal fun time. They both worked, and then one night, they went to the casino. She didn't play, but he did. He played cards, and she sat behind him to watch. They left late at night, and when they got home. it was the morning.

In the afternoon, they were headed to the car, and it was gone. My scared girl looked everywhere for it. She thought she parked in the wrong spot. No, her car was stolen. Seriously? Can't she get a break?

She called and filed a police report, and that was all she could do. Now, she needed a game plan. She still had to work. So she did, and she found ways to get to work without her car.

She continued to do so while she waited for her kids to come home from vacation with dad. They never came home. Deep down, she knew they weren't going to come home, but she couldn't do anything until that time had come and gone.

She called her attorney, and since my pissed-off heartbroken girl knew where the kids were at and the fact her ex-husband wouldn't just quit his job, she had to wait for them to come home. It was heartbreaking, and all she could do was work and come home and sleep. Her apartment looked like a hoarder's place. She refused to clean. She was exhausted.

There was a knock at the door. It was the sheriff. She was there for a welfare check. The hell? My broken girl explained that she didn't have her kids, that their dad had them. The sheriff wanted to come in and look around, so she granted entry. The sheriff found out the kids weren't there and proceeded to leave. My girl told the sheriff that her ex-husband took the kids on vacation and never came back, so this was a game by him. Apparently, the kids were now home, and when she didn't show up to pick up the kids, he called welfare check. What a dick. To make matters worse, the management team at her apartment complex was watching from the office window. Let's just say my girl's "kind" was not welcome in a fancy apartment complex.

Her attorney was not playing around with her ex-husband and filed for an emergency hearing, pretty much for being a dick. He never showed to the meeting. This worked out in my girl's favor.

She could get a ride to her ex-husbands house, and the sheriff was able to deliver an order to remove the kids from the home. Her ex-husband seemed confused on what was happening, but he was playing stupid to try and make my girl seem she has lost her mind. She did lose her mind, and she was pissed.

She couldn't believe that things had again gotten this bad. Her friends and family praised her for doing what she needed to do. She couldn't have done it without her love. She relied so heavily for his support, due to her fear of her family hurting her. She truly didn't trust anyone.

Court was set for a week after this incident. During the court hearing, he played dumb as though he didn't know he took the kids longer than usual. He blamed my girl for not picking up the kids and as well tried to blame her for not having transportation. She was working on it, but her car was stolen, and all her money was to provide for the kids. She wanted to be sure they were always taken care of.

Life wasn't good. There was a constant fear that something would happen to her kids. She was more worried about her son. She knew deep down her daughter would never be harmed. During all these court proceedings, my girl never tried to take the kids away from their dad, as far as losing custody. She just wanted him to stop being a dick.

One night at work, my girl received a phone call from the police department. They asked if she filed a report for a stolen car. She was so happy that they called. The police began to ask questions, which confused her. The outcome was this. Her ex-husband left his vacation with the kids, drove back down to her apartment, and took the car. He was still on the title, which my girl didn't remember. He sold the car legally since it was his.

When my girl made the police report, they thought it was to get back at him. The police had pulled over the new owners of the car and drew their weapons on them. A mom with a child in the back seat. The police explained how much trouble she can get into for lying. My girl explained that if she knew it was him, she wouldn't have made the report.

She told the police that she loved her job and could lose it if she knowingly did anything like this.

That was it, she was done, she wasn't going to let him get to her again. Ha! Lies, he will always hurt her—not really but this will last for years. Games, always with the fucking games.

My girl's dad, her hero, the one person in her family whom she is mostly alike, came over to visit with his love. Those two were her favorite people in the family. They were tough and told you to suck it up, but they loved fiercely and would do anything for their family.

They were just checking in with her and asked how she was getting to where she needed to be. She said she just did it. Friends, walking, whatever. It worked. Her dad had a bucket and handed it to her. In the bucket was car stuff. She didn't have a car. He told her he just got one and she could borrow it, but she needed to keep it nice. My grateful girl was so happy and appreciative, she started to cry.

She then found out the car was for her. She was blown away. It was a little SUV. Stick shift, her favorite. She loved her dad. He told her to not give up and that things would get better. This truck would be around for years and helped through so many different things in her life.

She and her love had to move. They couldn't afford the place anymore, and the management didn't want them being there anymore with all the visits from the sheriff's office. The next weekend, my girl and her love packed up the SUV with everything they had, including beds, and drove up the hill to her mom and stepdad's house. They would be there for about a month before they got their own place again. There were many fights in the house with her stepdad calling her love a loser because he couldn't take care of my girl in the way he felt she deserved.

My girl fought back. They weren't married, he didn't have to do anything. He chose to be there; he chose to help raise the kids. He chose to go to court and be supportive. He could have told her to kick rocks many times. There was nothing in common with the two of them that they would have to divide in court.

Instead of talking to her love, they would talk about him to her. She wasn't having it. He worked hard, and life happened. If that made him a loser, then she should have ended her life a long time ago. Fuck them.

My resourceful girl found a small apartment, just a one-bedroom, but it was something they could afford. Working in residential work was sometimes up and down, and she wasn't receiving child support yet.

In court, they had finally figured out an appropriate schedule for parenting and child support. The child support was going to help her breathe a little bit.

While her love worked, and she worked, this money would help with basic living. She didn't know where her mind was now, but her ex-husband wanted to meet with her privately to talk about the child support. She allowed him to manipulate her into reducing the child support by three hundred dollars. That didn't seem like a lot, but it was at the time. After everything he had done, she still let him manipulate her.

She didn't tell her love right away, since deep down she knew it was wrong—and no, she wasn't spending money on useless things. This money was to keep a roof over their heads and food on the table. Even to this day, she goes months without buying things for herself. She made her own money and would ask her love if she could buy a new pair of pants or even a cup of coffee. She had never gotten the abuse out of her head.

Both continued to work, and sometimes life got hard, money was hard. They couldn't get ahead. There were times when she and her love wouldn't eat and made sure the kids had food. She never wanted to go for assistance. She was too prideful.

I remember clearly one night, they used the last money that they had till payday and bought mac and cheese, sausage, and the cheap soda from Walmart. She didn't eat that day.

There were days when she would only eat at work; working in residential, that was a bonus.

Coming up was her brother's wedding. She was going to be a bridesmaid, and her sister-in-law and her mother were both bridezilla and momzilla. My girl was trying to be happy for her brother, but there were things that she couldn't participate in, due to finances. Luckily, she had enough for her dress.

Due to the custody arrangement, my girl had to give her ex-husband an itinerary of the wedding weekend, especially if it was in another county. Literally, this wedding was an hour drive, but she had to go through the hoops.

She and her love went to pick up her kids from school early on a Friday. She had a feeling her ex-husband would attempt the same thing and ruin the wedding for her brother. What her brother never knew, because he was so self-involved, was that the entire weekend, my protective girl had been on the lookout for her ex-husband to not ruin the wedding. Both her kids were in the wedding as well, and she put all the effort into making sure the kids would be there.

During the rehearsal, the MOB asked my girl if she remembered her Spanx to wear under her dress. My girl lost it. She got a dress that fit, and there was no way she was going to suck in her guts. Fuck you.

She ended up having fun for the most part. She felt beautiful in her dress, and her love looked very handsome. He filmed the wedding, which was nice, especially since he wasn't getting anything for it.

For all the fun that was had, the one part that my protective girl didn't find out till later was that her dad confronted her uncle for being a racist piece of trash. Her dad didn't stand for that shit. Her uncle had served his country, and apparently serving your country meant you can be a piece of shit. This isn't true for everyone, but for him it was. What a family she had.

During the wedding, there were a lot of drinking and dancing. My girl finally let herself go a bit. She had to. She had been so stressed, and for once, she was having fun.

Wedding weekend was over, and it was back to normal.

Work was going okay. Money was still a struggle when her brother and sister-in-law had a grand idea. They offered for all of them to live together to save money. This idea sounded good.

They moved in around the time school started again. It was only to be for a short time. During this time, my girl and her man were judged for everything under the sun. They would work and come home, make dinner for the kids, do homework. They didn't feel like socializing. But that wasn't appropriate in the good manners book.

Her love was looking for a better job, so it was just her working at the time. It was okay, things would get better, she knew it, and she just had to keep pushing forward.

Her sister-in-law would judge him. Coming up with some ridiculous things all the while treating her own husband like they were back in the fifties. Heaven forbid you took out the trash when it was full.

The moment my girl realized she wasn't family to them was the day her truck had broken down. Her love was doing errands, and the clutch went out. It was towed to an auto part store. My girl asked her sister-in-law, who was home with her, if she could use her car to go get him so he could grab the train and get to work. This trip would have been ten minutes, tops, round trip. Her response was "Sure, if I can get gas money, I'm trying to save on the mileage." Now before you judge her for getting upset, her sister-in-law had a gas-efficient car, and it wouldn't have used anything. Besides, this was family, and it was an emergency.

So, when my hurt girl went to pick up her love, they returned, and he literally threw money at her. Oh, and the kicker, she drove three hours away for a trip because she was stressed the very next weekend. So the ten minutes' round trip was too much, but you could leave for the next weekend? I mean it was your car, do what you wanted, but all the times you asked my girl and her love for help, they didn't ask for anything . . . not once. Because they felt they were family.

They ended up finding a house to rent by the end of the year. Both were so excited. The kids would have their own room, and they would be able to live peacefully. Things had finally calmed down with her ex-husband as well. Finally. Life was looking up. You would think so, right?

They lived in this house for over a year. That was the longest thus far.

Both my girl and her love worked hard; her love just got a new job opening a restaurant to be a bartender. My girl still worked in residential and was doing well. Kids were doing okay in school, and they went on doing the day-to-day routine.

The landlord was a slumlord, they found out later, and only cared about getting her rent. The house was older and had so much wood around it. There were spiders everywhere. One day, her love awoke with a bite on his abdomen. He kept an eye on it, but it kept getting worse. He went to the doctor, who they told him it was a bite. He had antibiotics. He began to have a fever and missed a few days of work. No eating and barely drinking.

My concerned girl was at work when her love called. He told her in so many words that he was thirsty and was in the kitchen getting water. He sounded delirious. He then said he spilled on him—*Oh no, wait, that is blood*, he said. The fuck? Blood! My scared girl asked him if he needed to call 911, but he said he was fine. Unfortunately, she was stuck at work, and yes, judgmental people, she should have left work right away; however, her love told her he was fine, and since there was only an hour left, she waited.

When she got home, as soon as she opened the door, there was nothing but blood. It was a crime scene. She walked down the hallway and followed the blood trail. He was on the bed, holding his abdomen with a washcloth. It was saturated. Enough of this shit, off to the doctor. As soon as they reached the doctor, they told him it was a Staph infection from the bite and he needed to go to the ER now.

The doctor pumped fluids in her love for hours and took this nasty white puss ball off his abdomen. Ever sit on leather seats in shorts and you stick to them? That's the sound it made.

They were in the ER from 6:00 p.m. to 7:00 a.m. It was a long night. My girl called her ex-husband and told him to keep an eye on the kids, just in case. He was going to keep them for the weekend so her love can get rest. It was a civil talk, and he said he wished him a speedy recovery.

After they were discharged, off to the store they went. If you didn't know he was just discharged from the hospital, one would think they were cleaning a crime scene. Gloves, bleach, trash bags—you name it, they bought it. They cleaned and disinfected the house for days. And my determined girl went and sprayed the house to get rid of anything that would hurt her family.

Family, what a concept. She loved this man to no end, and she knew deep down, things would be okay, but again her doubts were showing.

She wanted to get married to this man, and she had told him many times, but nothing. This would start huge fights that would end up with my sad girl feeling lonely. There was nothing that he did to say he didn't love her or wanted to be with her. These were her own insecurities. At one point, to make her happy he offered to leave and move back home. He just wanted her to be happy. She honestly didn't know what she wanted.

My girl has been sad and lonely since she was a child. She wore a smile that made the room light up. Her soul was damaged, and no one could fix it.

This was a lie; there was one person who could fix the damage. Her mom. All she ever wanted in life was to have her mom really dig deep and recognize the pain and betrayal, which was caused by her parents. My girl never wanted anything other than an apology.

She often wondered what would have happened in life all those years ago if her mom had believed her. Would she be strong, secure? Who knows?

While she went back and forth in her head about the trauma, her son was having issues again with his dad. One day, while my working girl was on shift, she received a phone call from her son's school. She normally couldn't leave work early, but she had no choice.

Her son was a freshman. My mama bear girl hated this school district and would continue to hate it. She arrived at the school and was brought into the principal's office. Her son's hair had been shaved, poorly, and he had a large bump on his head. He was also wearing clothes that were too small for him, and they were women's clothes. Everything in God's creation helped her to not kill her ex-husband.

She and her love took her son to the emergency room to get checked out. He was okay; ashamed but physically, he would be okay.

This was the final straw, and my mama bear girl won full physical custody of her son, but she and her ex-husband would share legal and medical. Her daughter would remain with the 50/50 custody.

Her daughter had never been hurt by her dad, and my girl wasn't going to take her away; there was no reason.

Over the next few years, life was getting better regarding work and home life. The one thing that wasn't getting better was her son.

He had the choice to go to his dad's or not, and there were times when he would and times he decided he wouldn't.

Her son had in his head that living with mom and her love would be fun, no rules. She bent them a bit due to the constant trauma.

Her son became manipulative and angry. To be honest, I think he was always that way, and he used his mom's love and her own traumas to take advantage of her. Her son was suspended from school for fighting with one of his friends. This was strike one. Three strikes, and he would be expelled from school.

In tenth grade, her son went to a new school. It was a technology-based school, they used iPads and had very fancy equipment. New school, new son—or so she thought. Her son had a girlfriend who was just as manipulative as he was. One day while at work, my working mama got a phone call from the principal's office again. This time, it was about her son damaging school property. A school meeting was to take place to figure out what was to be done. Strike two.

During the meeting, pictures were shows of the damage to the brand-new school. Her son had taken the iPad and slammed it against the wall. A piece of tile broke off. It was over $1,100 worth of damage. Her son laughed at his mom, who was in tears. He thought she would pay for it, and when she refused, he became vindictive and mean. The reason why he damaged property. His girlfriend was hugging her friend, who was a guy. She was hugging him because her son had yelled at his girlfriend, so she needed a friend to talk to.

This was the beginning of the end for the relationship with her son. At home, he wouldn't talk; he refused therapy. He was extremely mean and disrespectful. Even when his mom would attempt to do something nice for him, that wasn't good enough.

There were many times she felt bad for him and would give him what he wanted, not needed. He would become so ungrateful. The word *no* was used, but he didn't listen.

Everything came to a head one night when she and her son got in an argument. She couldn't take his behavior anymore and told him that if he couldn't follow the rules of the house and be respectful, then he would have to find a place to live.

He, to this day, will tell you she kicked him out. She told him his choices, and he chose. He ran away down the street to his friend's house. He called his grandfather, who was her stepdad, and all hell broke loose.

Her son told her he wanted to become emancipated and that he hated her. He couldn't even dress himself, and his hygiene was subpar. This was a joke, but he was serious. Things got bad from worse. He refused to come home, but she knew he was safe. She filed a report that he was a runaway.

This was what she did for a living, and now it was happening in her own home. Fuck this shit. When would it stop?

One day at work, she received an e-mail. It was a two-page e-mail going into detail about what a horrible mom she was, and that he didn't blame her because she didn't have a childhood and had to grow up so fast. He went into detail about how life would be better if it was just him, his sister, and my girl. He went into detail about how much he hated his own dad, and her love. The same love who protected him and loved him when he didn't even have to. She was devastated to read this.

Then she got to the part when he was showing signs of being suicidal. Immediately the plan was to pick him up early from school to have him assessed. During the assessment, he laughed at my scared girl and told him he knew how to get out of being admitted to the hospital. He was so confident in his actions. He wasn't admitted, but was told that outpatient therapy would suffice. Sure, it would. On their way home she, her love and her son stopped at the store to get groceries. He began to mock my exhausted girl in public. He would talk in her ear, and she tried to ignore it. He continued to tell her she was a horrible mom and that he didn't love her anymore.

Now, her love had always allowed her to deal with the kids and consequences because they weren't married. He always supported her and would guide her, but he wanted her to have the power. This time, however, he couldn't take it anymore and protected his love.

He said if her son was a real man to berate a female, someone who loved him, they would have words. It never got physical, but it was loud. They had an audience, but no one dared to interject. On the way home, her son sat behind her and threatened to hit her. She pulled over down the street from the house and told him to get out. She wasn't going to be put in danger, even if it was her son.

He never came home. He called his grandfather, and there it was decided by everyone but her that her son would live with his grandparents. He didn't like the rules set forth of being a decent human being, so he fought and manipulated his way up to living with his grandparents. The ones who originally wanted to adopt him when my sweet girl had him at the age of seventeen.

This is where the story gets good. What? You think that was it?

The decision to have her son up there was decided on by her ex-husband and her stepdad. Her mom swore she didn't have any-thing to do with it, but she could be in that category as well. This was to be temporary. A break. My smart girl warned everyone that if he left the house, he would not come back. She would let him, but if you ignored your problems and don't face them head on, eventually it got easier to not deal.

The difference between my girl and her son, she always tried to deal with her demons and was constantly shut down. She always continued to fight.

My strong girl needed some therapy. She knew Blue October was going to be in concert. She went with some friends and just sat and sobbed during the show. She thought of how her life had gotten this far and why shit always continued to happen. She wasn't a bad person. She was a caring person, sometimes too much. This concert helped her heal some wounds, but not all.

Over the span of a few months, life had calmed down. They didn't spend Christmas together, and that hurt. Life just kept going.

During family therapy sessions, there was nothing but hostility and yelling.

The goal was to "build" a relationship again, but how could you build a relationship if you weren't willing to work on your anger and own demons?

So my sad girl admitted defeat. She decided to go back to school, take care of her daughter, whom she had a great relationship with. Her love also found a great sales job, and with his other two jobs, they had plans to just be happy for a while.

Her love had to travel for his job, so he was gone a lot, and when he would come back, he would bartend. One shift bartending, he fell, landed wrongly on his foot, and he knew something was wrong, but he continued to work through his shift. It was over fourteen hours that he worked. He put his injury aside due to no one being there to cover. He finished his shift and iced his foot. Next day was Monday, before Monday-night football. He walked to work on his hurt foot and worked that shift. Over twelve hours. On Tuesday, he went to the doctors, and they told him his foot was broken. He was on the shelf. He didn't want to stop working. He didn't want to lose momentum. Due to his injury, her love couldn't work two out of the three jobs. He was stuck to doing the sales job. This worked for them.

The projected money would be great, and she was doing well at her job. Time went by, and it was noticed that the money wasn't coming in. Turned out, her love's boss was stealing money, and he never got paid for the deals he did.

Back to one income, but not for long. After everything was healed, her love found another bartending job, and then my sweet, loving girl was fired.

Before she was fired, she became the happiest girl. On Easter, her love asked her dad if he could marry her. They had already talked about it, but he wanted to be proper. The answer was "It's about damn time" And that was that. Her dad's love was extremely excited to help her plan for the wedding, which would be on their property.

Right after Easter, she was fired from a job she had literally poured her blood sweat and tears into.

At this moment, I am going to write about her job, it is time. This was the moment in life when my girl finally broke to pieces.

For years, she had worked with at-risk youth. She worked, sometimes so much, to protect and care for the broken that she wasn't at home—which now she feels that if she didn't work so much, her son would love her. No, her son never did, and it was constantly thrown in her face.

In the facility she worked at, there was a mixture of teen boys and girls. They slept in different cottages, which didn't stop them from having sex with each other. Each cottage had staff to watch over the kids. My girl was the supervisor on duty. She had her own team. Her team was bad as fuck. She trusted them with her life. The supervisor cottage was the girl's cottage. After their shift meeting, one of the male supervisors brought my girl into the office to show her a video he had found. The video was recorded months earlier.

The video showed two boys fighting. These boys were both kicked out of the program for not following the rules. The boy who recorded it was eighteen.

Knowing how this company treated their kids and staff, my boss lady girl attempted to have the eighteen-year-old boy remove the video. She tried for days. She didn't go to her boss right away because she thought he would be kicked out of the program. It was found out about the video, and was he kicked out of the program? No, because he was money. My boss lady girl and her two coworkers were. She was devastated. She wanted to flip the table and scream fuck you, but all she could do was sob.

Six years . . . and done . . . she was broken.

She did have another facility she worked at for her "fun" money. She was a supervisor and made minimum wage. It was shit, but again, she did it for the kids. It wasn't the same. Her heart wasn't in it anymore, but until she found something else, she pushed forward.

A month before her wedding, a riot broke out in her house she worked at. She was there from 3:00 p.m. to 8:00 a.m. the next morning. She had called the police a dozen times and tried to get the supervisor on duty to come to help. She didn't have her phone next to her, so it took a while. After the riot, which cost more than a month's pay for her, and with the smell due to the refrigerator being cleaned out all over she was done. She took leave. She was losing her mind.

She took a break to focus on the wedding. It was small. Twenty-five people max. There were many beautiful moments of that day. Her best friend was a witness, and her husband did the ceremony. My love's dad walked her down the aisle, which was a dirt path that they drove up to in her dad's classic cherry red Ford truck. Pure heaven!

They both wrote their own vows, and her love made the ladies cry. It was an amazing day.

All she ever has wanted was to be needed and loved. She didn't have the traditional bridesmaids, but her best friends were there. Her best friend was her witness. Most of her choices were sounded off by her girl. To her, having someone in her corner who didn't judge was what she needed most in life.

She had two other best friends. One my girl has known since the first grade, and while they are close, they went through long periods of not speaking. It was just who they are, but she was there to support my girl on her day.

Her other best friend flew in from another state. She made sure everything looked right for the wedding day. There were many times in life, she just needed a friend to tell her to shut the fuck up and to tell her she was being ridiculous. This was her; but at times, they were both being ridiculous.

Her mother-in-law was so excited because her son had found someone who loved him, no questions asked.

Then there was the other side.

Her son refused to apologize for anything, and he didn't come to the wedding. Her brother had deadlines and refused to come. And her mom was invited up to help set up for the wedding. Since it was at her dad's house, an invite wasn't needed, but it was just an extra gesture that she wanted her mom there. She didn't come till the wedding day. If she had known then what she did now, the guest list would have been massively different; it would have saved heartache.

She didn't let it ruin her day, and she and her love have not had a smooth marriage, but it's been all about love. All the stuff they went through was based off just life throwing bricks.

After her time off in between the riot and her wedding, she looked for jobs while she worked. She tried other residential facilities, but it didn't work out during the interview process.

She looked at going back to customer service, something she knew but she could clock in and clock out. Her soul hurt, but she kept on.

The job she found was a place she would frequent with her husband. Whenever they had a bad or good day, they would love to eat frozen yogurt, and one frozen yogurt place happened to be their favorite, right down the street.

All the employees were so nice, and the yogurt was amazing. After being around a company with no integrity, it was refreshing to see a company that did. She told her husband she could see herself working there.

She applied online and waited. She knew she was qualified for the job, but maybe overqualified. She just wanted a change. One night, she and her husband were there eating yogurt as usual, and the boss came over to talk to them. They had gotten to know him over time. She asked if he had received her resume, and they set up a time to sit down and talk.

She missed her first interview. She was in court for one of her clients at her home she worked at. It took all day, and there wasn't any way she would make it back in time. She did call in plenty of time, but she knew she blew it. First interview, really?

The next day, she went in to see if the boss was there. He was, and he gave her this look that read "You missed your first interview." She explained the situation, and he agreed to reschedule. All she wanted was a chance. She was early this time, and they spoke for a while. She had to go through the assistant, and they too spoke for a while. Even though she was qualified to be a manager, she wasn't qualified to manage this place. She knew nothing about frozen yogurt, except that it tasted good.

A few days later, she was at work when she received a phone call. It was the yogurt shop. They offered her a job as a Team Member, which was the very bottom. She was so happy and excited, but she remained professional when accepting. She didn't know asking for a chance for another interview would change her life for the better.

She finished working at the group home and was working part-time at the yogurt shop. She busted ass every shift. It was a breath of fresh air to work and go home and not worry about anything. Her first month she was there, she earned employee of the month. She was just doing her job.

As time went on, positions opened. First, it was a team supervisor position, then the assistant left, so that was open. She was still learning the team supervisor position, but she had manager experience, so she opened her mouth. After two and a half years, she became the store manager. All she did was put her head down and work, and she loves what she does.

In between starting to work there and her current title, life was amazing. It was perfect! Do you really think so? Not, it was those damn bricks.

While work for both were doing well, home life wasn't so good. They couldn't afford their place anymore. They both went from having great incomes to nothing. They had to downsize. They had to move again. One would think they should feel ashamed, but they didn't. They always tried their best at life, and shit happened.

Since they were downsizing, they gave themselves a year. So they put their stuff in storage and found a room to rent. Since they split time with her daughter, they figured one room would be sufficient. She and her daughter were super close, and her husband worked all the time. He had quit bartending and got a job at the local casino. It paid okay, but there were benefits, which they needed.

Her husband had found this place in a nice neighborhood. The house consisted of another couple and a middle-aged woman. My determined girl became friends with the girlfriend part of the couple of the house. She worked all the time and was just a sweet girl. The boyfriend of the couple treated her like shit and was lazy. That was all, and now we come to the middle-aged woman.

Unfortunately, the middle-aged woman had invited her daughter to stay in the house. Her daughter was mentally ill, who would do drugs and was a prostitute. Thankfully, my angry girl's daughter never found out. She wouldn't come around a lot, but when she did, the house was hostile. It got to the point where my girl would stay locked in her room with Netflix and her daughter. They were only there for a few months, due to the constant drama in the house caused by the middle-aged woman and her daughter.

With all the drama, it was causing my sweet girl so much stress. Her face and head would be in pain. The pain would last from minutes to hours. If you have had a migraine, you can relate.

She had to have an MRI to find out the problem, but of course, they couldn't find anything, and she had to beg the doctors to believe her.

Her entire body at times would itch, and she couldn't get rid of it. It was like she was on drugs herself. She just wanted to be normal.

The landlord didn't want to do the roommate situation anymore, and my girl and her husband couldn't blame him. He offered the house to them, but at the time, they couldn't afford it.

They moved in with her dad. This was different. She never moved back home with her dad before, but he was going to be gone for two weeks, and they would house-sit and stay and look for another place.

It was nice being at home. She found peace there. It's where she got married, and she was with the people who loved her most in the world and would protect her. They ended up staying from September to November. It wasn't a lot of time, but it worked.

They had found a studio, but it was in a house. Her husband wasn't interested at all, but her daughter wouldn't stop talking and saying how much she wanted to live there, and to be honest, my worried girl was scared her ex-husband would go back to his old ways. So they moved in. They lived there from November to August of the following year. It was okay living there. The main lady was the "boss." She had a husband who was pretty much her hired help. They liked him, but he was treated poorly. There was also an elderly lady who turned out to be a hoarder, and when it was found out that she was, my girl cleaned her room while she had to go to the hospital. All my girl's family wanted was to live in peace and work and save, but the longer they were there, the more "rules" were attached. Since it was month-to-month, when it was time to go, they did; but before they left, a milestone happened.

My sweet mama girl was invited to her son's graduation. She was overjoyed to go, and it was nice; he did work hard to graduate, but the happiness with her son didn't last long. Same kid, different age. Part of her believes he invited her to rub it in her face that he graduated. She only wanted what was best for him, always.

The moved out of the studio and found a sublease, which turned out to be a blessing, and from that, they were in a house by the landlord who rented out the sublease. This current house was only on a six months' lease, but it's been quiet, and they could think. During that time they had been at the current house, her husband got promotion, and so did she. They weren't living high on life, but they could afford gas in their car if they needed it without worrying if they had enough money for food. This had been the easiest living situation they ever had, besides the two months with her dad.

They had been excited to start over in a new place that wasn't for just a short time; they were excited to make her daughters room just how she wanted it and to be able to start her out in high school how it should be.

Since they moved into this current place, life has been fun, but on a budget. They were on a strict "need not want" basis, so that way they could afford to do what they needed to do. Never again did they want to not have money. It wasn't that they were irresponsible; it was just life kept throwing bricks.

My working mama was focused on her daughter and work—and of course, her husband—but being a mom was her greatest joy, even if things weren't as she wanted them. She held on to her daughter tight, but allowed her to be an individual.

She was finishing eighth grade, and it has been awful for her. Boys were teasing her, and she would come home sad and wouldn't talk. The counseling side of my mama girl came out, and she tried her hardest to get some answers to try and help. Nothing. She continued to support her daughter and would just be there with open ears and closed mouth, unless she needed to say something. They both were counting down the days till summer, and she could start her new school. The same school that her brother graduated from.

While being focused on her daughter, she was also focused on herself. She wanted people to know that she wasn't going to be stepped on anymore. This was hard for her because the people that hurt her were her own family—to be honest, just one complete side. These people would talk about her and her life behind her back but never asked her what was going on. It had been one big assumption after another.

Her stepdad invited her to lunch one day. She didn't know what to expect, but it was nice. She explained to him that she didn't hate anyone and that she was just doing her thing. She told him that all she ever wanted in life was to have people not kick her when she was down and to seriously acknowledge what happened to her as a kid.

Her stepdad asked why they never had any money, and she explained that as well. Her family thought they were just doing whatever the fuck they wanted. Why would it take so long to ask? That's my question.

A few weeks later, she and her mom had a talk. She apologized for being dismissive with her childhood. Her mom began to cry, and it was my strong girl who consoled her. The one who was abused didn't cry at all, and she told her mom everything would be okay.

My sensitive girl had this wall around her heart. It was solid, and the only way through was the ladder, to climb up one rung at a time. Her mom got one rung that day.

While my girl didn't trust her mom, it was a step, so it calmed her.

Life continued to go on, working and being a mom and wife. Her favorite things. Her daughter's troubles started to increase, so there was now going to be a change in class just for the last few weeks. Weeks can seem like eternity when you are dealing with any turmoil.

The point you know school was about to end was spring break! My working mama had so many plans to spend with her daughter.

Knott's and one of the animal parks. Movies and nails. She had been saving money to do this, and she was sure she took time off to spend with her. They both needed it, to just relax.

Her stepdad asked if her daughter could spend a few days up with them and then bring her home on my girl's days off. That plan worked. Even though she didn't have the best relationship, she would never keep her daughter away from her grandparents. It's never fair to use kids like that.

When her daughter came home, she was dropped off at my girl's work. She wanted nothing to do with her mom. This was odd because she loved her mom. That night, silence; and her mom began to worry. She didn't know what to do. She confiscated her daughter's phone for the night to see if that would help, but she locked herself in her room. Early the next morning, my concerned girl went through her daughter's phone.

Her heart broke, shattered more than anything in her life. Both her son and daughter had been talking through text messages about their mom and her love. They went on for quite a while about how horrible of a mom she was and how they couldn't stand her love. Here was the kicker, her daughter never acted this way toward them. Her brother went on to tell her that they could live together and he would buy her stuff, or if she really couldn't stand to be with her mom, then she could live with her dad because he was a good dad.

The dad, whom her son had once accused of abusing him, that started all this fucking shit in the first place.

My girl lost it and began to sob. Her daughter? No emotion. She looked at her as though she was a stranger crying, not her mom who had done nothing but love, guide, and support her in anything. All my girl wanted was her daughter to grow up to be a decent person who valued other people, just like her mama did.

My girl called her best friend, who came over, and her husband left so that way she could have some girl time. Her best friend was at a loss and could only sit with her while her daughter sat and stared at her mom.

My girl called her ex-husband as well and asked him if he knew anything. While she believed he didn't know anything, I know he didn't feel bad for her. She was getting what he went through. The difference was she had never laid a hand on her daughter like he did their son.

They both spoke, and my crushed girl told him she would let her decide where she wanted to live; the reason being was that she was at the legal age, and even though she knew deep down this was manipulation by her son, she was allowing it to not further strain the relationship she thought was intact.

She tried telling her mom and stepdad about what happened and their response was *Sorry that happened, it must hurt, but sorry we can't talk about it right now.* It took two weeks for them to even check in on their own daughter to see if she was even alive because of this building that had fallen on her head.

She went numb.

She dusted herself off and went to work the next day and the day after that. Not many people knew about her daughter, but the people who did and mattered were trying to support my girl as best as they could.

For two weeks, there were random texts messages between my girl and her daughter. These were more of requests of things her daughter wanted, not needed but wanted.

The Sunday before Mother's Day, my sad girl's husband had gotten her meet-and-greet tickets to see her favorite band, Blue October. I can go on for hours about how much my girl loves them and how this band and their music has saved her life many times. When she finally came face to face with the band, she teared up. She thanked them for helping her through all her trauma. Without them, she would either be dead or addicted. Those who heal from music completely understand this.

The show was extremely therapeutic for her, and she could be at peace with life for a while.

Mother's Day was to be on her weekend, and she was talking to her daughter again through text message to get an idea if she was coming over. She knew deep down her daughter wasn't going to come over, but she wanted to hear it. Her daughter told her she needed something from my broken girl and that was why she wanted to see her. She held in the tears; she wasn't going to cry. She built the wall higher.

On Mother's Day, my girl's husband, her love, her best friend did whatever she wanted. She cried in the shower and went on her day. All day, she was focused on why she was a shit mom, daughter, and sister. The only people to acknowledge her that day were her husband, dad, and dad's love.

My girl, knowing this wasn't her fault, again thought of herself as trash. The cycle continued.

Do you think there is more? Not now, and who knows what is going to happen to my girl.

She will continue to get up and push forward, and maybe one day, she will find out why God wants her here, because right now she is damaged and confused.

I will hopefully have an update for you soon, and even though I don't have a soul, I'm exhausted talking about how messed up my girl is. I'm sure there was something I could have done to protect her. No wings for me. After all, I'm an asshole.

See you on the other side.

# My Ending: But Not Really

T his project took so much of myself to complete. There was a lot of my life that I left out, or you would have been reading for the rest of your life. I had to take myself out of the writing because it hurt too much, so this was where Harry came into play. I fully believe I have had an angel watching over me. A very bad angel but nonetheless.

You are probably wondering if I hate people. No, I don't. It's not in my nature.

I appreciate all the heartache and love. It makes me who I am.

However, I have always wondered what would have happened in my life if I just had someone who protected me, who loved me enough to say, *That wasn't okay, and we will do what we can to make sure you heal.* Then again, there have been so many wonderful things in my life that started from this mess that was called my childhood.

# About the Author

Tara grew up in beautiful San Diego. Her heart belongs in San Francisco. Not only is Tara an avid reader, she has been writing since she found out her mind has more to offer than the words will fit on paper. Tara spent most of her adult life thus far working with at-risk youth in a community setting. Now she manages a frozen yogurt shop, which gives her more time to spend on activities which make her happy. Tara is very passionate about life and justice. Tara will not stop seeking answers to questions until she is satisfied. Tara is a survivor of domestic violence and sexual assault. Tara is very outspoken about her life to attempt to help others who have similar backgrounds heal. Due to Tara's traumatic past, she suffers from depression and anxiety and PTSD. Tara also suffers from trigeminal neuralgia, a nerve disorder that affects her face in a very painful way.

Tara is a mom of two beautiful children who are following their own path in life; her love for them is unconditional.

Tara is married, and she and her husband both enjoy watching sports and television shows together. Tara is constantly supported by her husband to follow her dreams. During basketball season, you can always catch Tara watching her Golden State Warriors, and in her spare time, she is listening to music and reading. Tara reads a book a week in order to keep up with her large book collection.

CPSIA information can be obtained
at www.ICGtesting.com
Printed in the USA
FSHW04n2040230418
47366FS